i, the citizen

Balu offers a perspective of development and better life from where the reality of these questions is actually lived, and not from a distant perch. Often agonizing, equally often inspiring, and always real, this book is the next best thing to going and working with Balu in the forests of Heggadadevanakote.

ANURAG BEHAR
Chief Sustainability Officer of Wipro Limited;
CEO of Azim Premji Foundation, and Vice Chancellor, Azim Premji University, India

This book presents an exceptional and inspiring narrative, not only of Dr. Balu's story but also the stories of many citizens. One need not agree with all of Dr. Balu's views to share his essential commitment to human betterment.

GARY FIELDS
John P. Windmuller Professor of International and Comparative Labor and Professor of Economics, Cornell University, USA

Coming from an eminently qualified individual to tell us what development really means both in theory and practice, this book is a 'must-read' for activists, researchers, development practitioners, civil servants and policy advocates.

S K DAS
Former Secretary to the Government of India, Honorary Advisor to Indian Space Research Organization and author

Dr. R. Balasubramaniam is a visionary whose aim in life is to make the voice of the voiceless to be heard. He reminds me of William Wiberforce who, as a young MP in the House of Commons, started the "Anti-Slavery movement" in 1807, and carried on with it even when his friends told him that he was breaking his head on a rock and when there were threats to his life. He won at the end and the Anti-Slavery Bill was passed in 1833 three days before his death. His efforts are one of the greatest contributions to mankind.

The experiences of the villagers depicted in the book reveals how, in this world the powerful-monetary, muscle or political power-want to make the rich richer and the poor poorer. Only a committed set of people, small in number to begin with can build a tsunami of change. I hope this wonderful book starts the whirlwind for change.

PROF. B M HEGDE
Padma Bhushan awardee, Former Vice Chancellor of Manipal University, India; Medical scientist, educationist and author

I, the Citizen *discards clichés and jaded thought, and brings in a fresh vocabulary, a new insightful discourse on development. Drawing wisdom from the past and the present, the book offers a framework for the future – in which people are the protagonists, and people's role in governance, pivotal.*

T V NARENDRAN
Managing Director, Tata Steel and Chairman of Confederation of Indian Industry, Jharkhand

Part call to action, part memoir, I, the Citizen demonstrates the power of citizen engagement through a series of humbling parables that reveal Dr. Balu's lifelong commitment and seemingly enduring faith in the potential of India and humanity.

LAURA SPITZ
Vice Provost for International Affairs, Cornell University, USA

Dr. Balu is the quintessential activist and true global citizen who seeks justice and truth. Whether the cause is fighting corruption, arguing for a rural jobs program, teaching the poor on their right to know, or helping to draft legislation around corporate and social responsibility, he nourishes the most basic principles and practices of a free and democratic society. As our world becomes more complex and dangerous, it is people like Balu and his book, I, the Citizen, that will help inspire each of us to take up a small part of Balu's struggle.

JOSEPH GRASSO
Associate Dean for Finance, Administration, and Corporate Relations, Cornell University, USA

i, the citizen
unraveling the power of citizen engagement

DR. R BALASUBRAMANIAM

Foreword by **Justice M N Venkatachaliah** Former Chief Justice of India

Published in association with Cornell University Press

This book was made possible, in part, by a generous grant from Joseph Grasso in recognition of Dr. Balasubramaniam's long and fruitful relationship with him and Cornell University.

First published in Mysuru, India in 2015 by Grassroots Research and Advocacy Movement (GRAAM), CA-2, KIADB Industrial Housing Area, Ring Road, Hebbal, Mysuru 570016 India. citizen@graam.org.in

First published in the United States of America in 2017 in association with Cornell University Press

Library of Congress Cataloging-in-Publication Data

Names: Balasubramaniam, R., 1965– author.
Title: I, the citizen : unraveling the power of citizen engagement / Dr. R. Balasubramaniam ; foreword by Justice M.N. Venkatachaliah, former Chief Justice of India.
Description: Ithaca, New York : Published in association with Cornell University Press, 2017. | "First published in Mysuru, India in 2015 by Grassroots Research and Advocacy Movement."
Identifiers: LCCN 2017011966 (print) | LCCN 2017015447 (ebook) | ISBN 9781501712470 (pdf) | ISBN 9781501712463 (epub/mobi) | ISBN 9781501713514 (pbk. : alk. paper)
Subjects: LCSH: Political participation—India—Tsundur.
Classification: LCC JQ281 (ebook) | LCC JQ281 .B357 2017 (print) | DDC 323/.042095485—dc23
LC record available at https://lccn.loc.gov/2017011966.

Editing: Rohit Shetti
Illustrations: Mara B and Manoj Kalkar
Layout and typesetting: Deepak Mote

Cornell University Press strives to use environmentally responsible suppliers and materials to the fullest extent possible in the publishing of its books. Such materials include vegetable-based, low-VOC inks and acid-free papers that are recycled, totally chlorine-free, or partly composed of nonwood fibers. For further information, visit our website at cornellpress.cornell.edu.

I dedicate this book to all my activist friends who have stood up to the cause of citizenship over the past few decades, and to all my indigenous friends and chieftains for welcoming me into their lives and for teaching me so much.

CONTENTS

Information indeed is power – people and their right to information

Citizen engagement and the fight against corruption

Citizen engagement towards making democracy work

ACKNOWLEDGMENTS

Writing has been both a passion and a sanity-preserving exercise for me. I started writing a little more than eight years ago and have been expressing my views on different matters through my blog. I have also maintained that I wrote not for an audience, but more for myself. This logic can indeed be very uninspirational. What I needed was someone to goad and push me to actually complete a manuscript and make the work publishable. This would not have happened without the support of my friend Rohit Shetti who helped edit and shape the earlier Indian edition of this book. Joseph Grasso, the Associate Dean for Finance, Administration, and Corporate Relations at the ILR School, Cornell University, and a very good friend, suggested that this book should reach a wider global audience. I thank him for not only taking the manuscript to the team at Cornell University Press but also for supporting the publication of the book in more ways than one.

Justice M N Venkatachaliah, the former Chief Justice of the Supreme Court of India, has been a mentor, guide, and an extraordinary source of inspiration for me throughout my career. I thank him for writing the foreword to this book. I would also like to thank Manoj and Mara, both of them former students of Viveka Tribal Center for Learning, a school for forest-based tribal children in the forests of Heggadadevanakote, Mysuru, for giving an artistic expression for my thoughts.

This edition of the book would not have been possible without the support of Dean Smith, Director, Cornell University Press, and his team. Their patience and hard work at editing the manuscript and making it publishable in such a short time is indeed impressive. I thank them and Laura Spitz, Vice Provost for International

Affairs, Cornell University, for not only reposing confidence in me but also for ensuring that this book be published.

All events and life incidents narrated in this book actually took place. If it had not been for everyone involved in these occurrences, I would have neither learned as much nor had anything to write about. I thank my colleagues, friends, and indigenous brethren for being what they are and giving so much to society in general and to me in particular. I also wholeheartedly thank my fellow travelers at the Swami Vivekananda Youth Movement (SVYM) and Grassroots Research and Advocacy Movement (GRAAM), India, for the faith they have had in me, in themselves, and in the power of common citizens, and for the many lessons in the grassroots approach to development that we discovered together every passing day.

I am indebted to hundreds of people from all walks of life—activists, corporate executives, street vendors, government officials, politicians, professional and academic colleagues, and students—who have made an impact on my development journey so far. I thank them for their faith in the process of citizen engagement and in me.

The book would not have seen the light of the day but for the support, encouragement, and love that my wife, Bindu, shows me despite all my faults, and the affection and spirit of accommodation that my son, Aniruddh, has shown to create the time and space for me to work. I am deeply thankful to them for making my life worth living.

Dr. R Balasubramaniam

Mysuru, India, June 2017

FOREWORD

Dr. R Balasubramaniam or Balu, a physician by qualification and a humanist by instinct, lives a unique life in our times. He keeps his pace to a different drummer and has an instinctive discrimination of what true human development is and what masquerades as one. Having spent a good part of his life living and working in remote tribal colonies, he is able to appreciate and bring forth grassroots perspectives about development, while also having sound understanding of the dimensions of policy making from the point of view of a top level bureaucrat.

The world of policy making itself is riddled with many challenges and is getting murkier by the day with unabashed lobbying by vested interests, who unfortunately seem to be gaining an upper hand. Yet, Balu has not let go of his faith and belief that people's participation and community voice must find space in the way policies are framed and implemented, regardless of the ideologies of those in power. In 'I, the citizen', he revisits the familiar debate about the once famous 'trickle-down' theory of progress in the backdrop of what may be termed as democratic processes of development and the space it provides for citizens to engage.

The famous maker of modern Singapore, Lee Kuan Yew, who passed away in March 2015 had propounded what is known as the Lee Thesis, wherein democracy is considered to be an impediment to development. Of course, development here largely refers to economic growth, a kind that Human Development Reports have described as "ruthless, rootless, jobless, voiceless and futureless". It is high time that the governments understood that only investment in social welfare measures such as education, health-care, and social security is a sure source of enduring benefits. The concern however is that these areas are dwindling in the radar of government's priorities.

Today's concept of development is GNP and GDP oriented. These numbers are ethic neutral and lack moral content. Illegal or even criminal activity could produce economic results and enhance the GNP. Moreover, impressive numbers can even be achieved by vesting controls only in the hands of a few, a trend that is already visible. In such a scenario, it is only a citizen uprising that can be trusted upon to bring about corrective action. This uprising need not be in terms of revolts and protests, but in constantly expanding the role and scope of citizens to engage in governance and administration and to demand transparency and accountability.

Amartya Sen in his book 'Development as Freedom' defines development as a process of expanding the real freedoms that people enjoy. The 'expansion of freedom' itself is viewed as the primary end as well as the principal means of development. An important lesson about development we must learn is that economic growth does not trickle down, and that big-ticket investment does not guarantee enhancement of the quality of life of people. Thus, it is essential to de-link development from economic growth. In fact, the Report of the Commission appointed by the French President on "Measurement of Economic Performance and Social Progress" indicates the inadequacy of the concept of "GDP" to capture some essential components of 'development' when distinguished from mere 'growth'.

Macroeconomic stability is essential and human needs must be met by specific state interventions, but 'social preparedness' is a prerequisite for the results to be meaningful, even if they are of economic dimensions. No one policy will suffice to bring about holistic development by itself; a comprehensive approach to development needs to be adopted with the support of institutional arrangements. This entails that public goods such as education, health, human security must be regarded not as rewards of development, but as essential to the very process of development.

Sen further speaks of differing attitudes to the process of development. "One view sees development as a "fierce" process, with much "blood, sweat and tears" - a world in which wisdom demands toughness. In particular, it demands calculated neglect of various concerns that are seen as "soft-headed" (even if the critics are often too polite to call them that)." "This hard-knocks attitude contrasts with an alternative outlook that sees development as essentially a "friendly" process. Depending on the particular version of this attitude, the congeniality of the process is seen, as exemplified by such things as mutually beneficial exchanges (of which Adam Smith spoke eloquently), or by the working of social safety nets, or of political liberties, or of social development-or some combination or other of these supportive activities." Development economists such as Prof. Jean Drèze also observe that human capabilities are as important as physical capital for economic growth and the quality of life. Continuing with policies that consider growth and development as synonymous, where human capital takes a back seat hence may be termed regressive.

Balu, as I know him, is fiercely passionate about looking at development as an expansion of capabilities and more importantly, this view is not one acquired from books or from emulating leading thinkers, but evolved through three decades of being in the thick of development processes and observing what works and what kind of development lasts. This book contributes to the discourse on development by taking one through these experiences and reflections thereof.

Will Durant called civilization a social order which promoted cultural creations constituted by four elements – economic provision, political organization, moral traditions and the pursuit of knowledge and the arts. The non-physical and non-economic dimensions of the idea of development, the famous and multisplendored embellishments of Indian cultural life namely art, architecture, sculpture, music, drama, painting and astronomy of the highest perfection were inspired by noble aesthetic values. There are also lesser recognized values, world views, traditions and culture of the indigenous people rooted in the very nature amidst which they have lived, but are now under threat as the march of 'development' challenges their survival. These are values that the 'mainstream' may well learn and adopt for the greater good of mankind. The author brings out cultural dimensions of development in this book in the form of grassroots perspectives of development, leadership lessons and values gained from having lived with the indigenous communities for more than two decades.

Dr. Balasubramaniam, not just through his writing, but through his work has touched a live-wire in the current discourse on which kind of development process is best suited to India. It is a timely caution to us that we may after-all not be treading the best path. An initiative called GRAAM is inquiring into this under his leadership and is trying to bring grassroots evidences and people's voices closer to the policy planners, which may help us chart our course as a nation wisely, guided by the framework of the Indian Constitution.

In essence, "We, the people…" the words at the beginning of the Preamble to the Constitution of India are not different from "I, the citizen". Both call for reflection and action from all of us to make sure that democracy evolves into something better than it already is, and India as a nation can be a testimony to the world about how democracy and development can indeed be compatible.

M N Venkatachaliah
Bengaluru

PREFACE

In my experience of over thirty years, I have found that 'development' is defined by different people based on their own 'expertise' and the way their perspectives have been shaped. When I started my own development journey, I held the predominant and narrow view that development equates to growth in income, expansion of infrastructure and rise in the standard of living. Over time, United Nations and other agencies began differentiating between 'growth' and 'development' and people had begun to reassess what 'development' could really be and mean. My own views were being tested day in and day out by ground realities and exposure to new socio-political dynamics.

Most communities that I lived and worked with had their own established grassroots interpretation of development and the various processes that facilitated or inhibited it. My views on development and its processes began to be shaped and reshaped by the direct experience of working and partnering with communities. The identity I assumed for myself about being a 'provider' was being challenged constantly and I had begun engaging with people and communities with the humility of a 'partner'. It took efforts to reconcile textbook theories with the complexities of a rapidly changing society, in which I was also trying to find my feet as an action-oriented development practitioner.

Years later as I began reflecting on these dynamics, I realize that most development practitioners continue to have pre-packaged ideas on how to 'develop' people and are often un-prepared for field realities that exist. This patronizing attitude is not only flawed and misplaced but also contributes to wastage of precious and scarce resources. My own learning began only when I decided to 'listen' and hold back my interpretations and conclusions, and it involved a fair bit of unlearning. I learned that I had to first identify with the people I was working with and that interventions are more relevant when their need and scope emerge through a collective process. This also allowed me to recognize, and often marvel at the untapped wisdom and knowledge inherent in indigenous tribal and rural communities.

My study and stay at Harvard University gave me an invaluable and unique opportunity to re-interpret many of my experiences. Amidst the most celebrated academicians in the world, I could validate many of my undertakings as a practitioner. There was a fair share of negation of what I did as well; a lot of wisdom and learning that one may find among communities and people at the grassroots level hardly found place in formal academic environments.

I felt the need to capture these invaluable 'voices from the grass-roots' and share the narratives with a larger audience, and therefore I started a blog. The blog also provided me space to articulate my re-interpretations of the development journey I had begun in the eighties and see them in today's context. I not only attempted to capture the wisdom and perspectives of the communities, but also my own learning and interpretations from them. Then there were responses to current happenings in the world, campaigns that we undertook and articles on development, politics, governance, public policy and democracy that found space in the blog. This entire process coincided with a period where my conviction about how powerful and meaningful citizen engagement can be, has increased and continues to increase. A deep faith in the relevance and validity of the Indian Constitution, one of the finest blueprints for social re-engineering ever crafted by the human mind, further authenticated my conviction.

This book is a result of encouragement by friends and readers who received the blog well, and strings together the largely independent articles into a volume that consolidates my reflections and perspectives on development, policy and citizen engagement. The book contains articles that capture the meaning of development as seen and interpreted by different people that I have come across, and how they contributed to my own learning and growth. My experiences of engaging with people in civic action have been pivotal in furthering my belief in citizen engagement and naturally constitutes a major chunk of the book. I have also tried to present my outlook on certain policies and my observations on governance and democracy today. Lastly, through a set of fresh reflections, I have attempted to trace how citizen engagement remains an unending movement through some momentous initiatives of the organizations that I have founded and led.

Citizenship and citizen engagement may have a different and more comprehensive definition in the academic circles than that identified in this book. This is neither a book laying out theoretical perspectives nor is it a guidebook that provides a toolkit for citizenship and citizen engagement. What it does contain is an interpretation of citizenship evolved from directly working in the field, with people's movements and interactions with thousands of everyday individuals as well as several local leaders, activists, politicians, bureaucrats and students. I have understood that citizen engagement is about collaborative partnerships and dialogue of which confrontation is also a component. It is about inclusion, empowerment, and mutual accountability and is undoubtedly a political process.

Further, the first step of meaningful citizen engagement in development is citizens' claim for their legitimate civic space. This in itself is a challenging process and requires civil society and the government to back communities in their pursuit of making their voice heard. I have learned from leading and involvement in people's campaigns and from working with and constantly negotiating with the government that there is a lot of ice that needs to be broken. The positive news however is, that there is evidence to show that communities are keen on enhancing their participation around the world. A technology enabled community monitoring initiative conceived, designed and implemented by a team at GRAAM has helped me appreciate how technology can help create and expand the space for effective civic engagement. Practical experience and working as a consultant with multi-lateral agencies like the World Bank also taught me that citizen engagement should not be viewed as a duel between the citizen and the state, but as two complementary forces working together to ensure overall development of a community or a nation. One must appreciate that the evolution of citizen engagement is the evolution of democracy itself. Anecdotes in this book will help the reader understand how citizen engagement can strengthen governance processes, deepen democracy, and help in not just overcoming income poverty but also in overcoming 'voice' poverty and social exclusion.

I hope that this book will serve to bring in a different perspective in the minds of development practitioners, social activists, politicians, government officials and students of social work. My hope is that it will encourage them to understand that true development can only be achieved when there is a partnership based on mutual respect, trust and dignity among stakeholders accompanied by a genuine desire to make a positive change in this world. If the ideas and experiences in this book fosters a dialogue on the very nature of development, its purpose is well served. The onus is on us to turn technology and globalization into forces that deepen democratic values, empower communities and fight inequities through civic action. The power of citizen engagement can change the process of development as we know it. Development, by the people and for the people is indeed possible.

Dr. R Balasubramaniam (Balu)
Mysuru

"ALL THAT IS VALUABLE IN HUMAN
SOCIETY DEPENDS UPON THE
OPPORTUNITY FOR DEVELOPMENT
ACCORDED THE INDIVIDUAL."

ALBERT EINSTEIN

Understanding development

Development is a buzzword that has been used and abused to shape the political and economic dimensions of entire nations. It is projected as a broad purpose and justification of all activities, often without answering the questions of whose development and how. Having been a development practitioner for three decades, while also wearing the hat of a academician, leadership consultant and policy advocate at times, I have not yet arrived at a precise definition of development. The experience has certainly helped me evolve my understanding of development and appreciate the fact that it has multiple dimensions. It is also evident that people have different perspectives about development and it is more important to comprehend what it truly means and feels like to different people than just to define the term. My belief that development is a constant expansion of human capabilities and that it must result in the creation of human and social capital to be meaningful has only strengthened over the years.

This introductory section comprises articles that articulate different facets of development and what it means to different people and agencies. More importantly, it is embedded with questions and perspectives that I hope, can help critique the current paradigm of development and help us evolve our understanding of the phenomenon.

Defining development and its path

Sahebganj is a district in the central-eastern state of Jharkhand bordering West Bengal. It was part of the Santhal Parganas[1] and is mostly inhabited by indigenous tribals. It is the only district in Jharkhand through which the river Ganga flows. During the British Raj[2], most of the Englishmen lived around the railway station and hence the town and the district got to be known as Sahebganj or the 'place of the Sahebs[3]'. More than a decade ago, I had the opportunity of traveling through the scenic Rajmahal hills located in this district. I was on an assignment for the World Bank trying to understand the problems of malaria in that region and being deeply concerned about tribal issues, I had opted to focus on the hilly and difficult areas in which they lived.

The experience of one particular afternoon is still fresh in my mind. It was around lunch time and I was in a village inhabited by the Mal Paharia, one of the primitive tribal groups living in Jharkhand since time immemorial. I decided to visit one of the homes close by. I knew that rice was their staple food and was hoping that I would be offered some by the lady of the house. As

1   Santhal Paraganas was a district in Bihar before the state of Jharkhand was carved out of it in 2000. Santhal Paragana is now one of the 5 administrative divisions of Jharkhand state.

2   British Raj or The Raj refers to the period between the mid-nineteenth century and independence of India in 1947 during which the British ruled and colonized most of the Indian subcontinent.

3   The Englishmen were often addressed as Sahebs, which translates to Sir or Master, especially by those communities that had to be subservient to them.

I entered the house, I noticed three young children playing on the floor and a woman cooking on a mud hearth. She was breast-feeding a six month old baby as she continued cooking, while I noticed another child around two years old, sleeping on the floor beside her. With the help of a local translator who spoke the version of Bengali that this woman spoke, I gathered that these five were her children. Her husband had gone out in search of work and food, and was expected later that evening.

My first reaction as a doctor was to feel concerned that this young woman who was no more than twenty-five years of age, and looked much older, had five children already. The older children clearly looked malnourished and I was curious to know what she was cooking for them. She had made some rice and was preparing a watery gravy to be eaten with the rice. Vegetables were a luxury for this family and she had put in some leafy greens that she had picked in the forest nearby. I learned painfully that this constituted the main meal on most days and she would eat what was left after feeding her older children.

Continuing the conversation, I soon learned that neither health-care nor education had reached anywhere near their village though both the government and local NGOs claimed that they had indeed created access for these services. This simple tribal woman had accepted her life as it came and her only pre-occupation seemed to be finding the next meal for her children.

Though this scene left me agitated, I noticed a peculiar calm on the woman's face; she seemed unperturbed by her socio-economic condition. It sounded ironic that though governments, civil society groups, development experts and donor agencies were talking about food security, creating access to health, education and other public services and ensuring social and economic justice for these margin-alized people, here was a Mal Paharia tribal family untouched by either the debate or the 'benefits' of such development interventions.

Recollecting this incident still leaves me confused and

disillusioned about what really constitutes 'development'. Is it about providing health, education, food, nutrition, livelihood, water and sanitation, roads and other infrastructure or is it something more? Is it about paving way for a more dignified life for this Mal Paharia family? Or is it about technological advancement and sending missions to the Mars or the Moon? Is it about taking this family's aspirations beyond securing the next meal? Or is it some abstract statistic?

The debate on development has intensified over the last three to four decades; it gathered much momentum after the United Nations made the grand announcement of the Millennium Development Goals (MDGs). Eight international development goals were officially established following the Millennium Summit of the United Nations in 2000 following the adoption of the United Nations Millennium Declaration. All 193 United Nations member states and at least 23 international organizations agreed to achieve these goals by the year 2015.

We are in 2015 and it does not take an expert to tell us that the world is far from achieving these goals. And it is only in the last couple of years that the United Nations and NGOs around the world have woken up to the fact that these goals were ambitious and that enormous sums of money in numerous programs have been spent. There are concerned voices from civil society demanding that the programs launched to achieve these goals should not be terminated after having reached the deadline of 2015. There are other voices that are urging a rethink on the development goals themselves, given the changing contexts.

Rethinking and redefining development goals is indeed needed, but it must also be accompanied by a rethinking of how these goals shall be achieved. We are at that cusp in the history of mankind where we could ruinously pursue a path of economic growth that leaves millions of families like the ones in Sahebganj in the lurch or choose a more democratic and inclusive path which accounts for the voices of these families. Priorities must be reset to stem the growth of inequity, and communities must be at the center of the development agenda that nations pursue.

As a nation, we would do well to remember the words of Amartya Sen, who said "India should not hope for the social benefits of economic progress, but rather look towards the economic consequences of social progress." We need to appreciate that development has to result in a constant expansion of human capability. The question really is whether we have the belief, courage and tenacity to translate this vision of development into a concrete reality where the rule of law is the norm rather than the exception, where no family will go hungry, where human rights is not a mere slogan but a way of life, where democratic participation is not a fanciful aspiration but an everyday expression of citizenship, and where food, nutrition, livelihood, infrastructure, education, healthcare and religious freedoms are not mere political promises but rights of an empowered citizenry. And it is not the lawmakers or bureaucrats or policy advocates who need to carry this belief or demonstrate the courage. It must begin with and involve ordinary citizens who believe in collectively demanding and working towards a process of development, whose outcomes are relevant to them and reflect their aspirations.

Who defines development?

It was 1988. It had been little more than a year since I had started a new chapter in my life amidst the indigenous tribal communities in a hamlet named Brahmagiri, adjoining the Bandipur National Park in the southern Indian district of Mysuru. We had just started a dispensary and I used to spend most of my mornings at the clinic, while the afternoons were reserved for visiting the nearby tribal colonies for interacting and getting to know the people and their contexts better. I was on one such visit to Rajapura tribal colony and was talking to the women there. During the conversation, I learned that these women walked nearly eight to ten kilometers every day to fetch water from the nearby Kabini River. I was aghast on hearing this. I was disturbed by the thought of these long walks and the amount of time that the women spent every day just to get water for their households. The plight of these women was an unacceptable situation to me and I told myself that I must do something about this.

A few days later, I met the Chief Secretary of the Zilla Panchayat, a position now known as the Chief Executive Officer, then the highest ranking official of the district administration, and explained to him the situation in Rajapura and the need for a tube-well with a hand-pump in the tribal colony. He was sympathetic to my plea and responsive too, and had a tube-well with a hand-pump erected within the next week or so. This meant that water was now available in close proximity to the homes of the community. I felt extremely happy that the problem of water was solved and the women of Rajapura did not have to walk these long distances, spending at least three hours on each trip to fetch water from the river.

Days passed by and work at the dispensary in Brahmagiri kept me busy along with the work related to the Swami Vivekananda Youth Movement, an organization that I had founded in 1984. It was only about six months later that I was able to visit Rajapura again. I went there expecting to receive the adulation of a grateful community for reducing their workload and making their lives better; for having helped the women overcome one of their day-to-day hardships, and for the stride in development that the community took.

I wasn't prepared for the surprise that awaited me. On reaching Rajapura, I was received with the choicest expletives from the women, who were visibly angry upon seeing me. Bommi and Madi, the most vocal among them made no attempts to hide their displeasure or disappointment. I simply could not understand why these women were upset with my attempt to help them get a source for collecting water virtually at their doorstep. It was as baffling as it was disheartening.

On probing, I understood the real impact of what I had done. These women were upset with me because I had taken away what was very valuable to them. Fetching water from the river was the only time that they could get away from their homes, families and their husbands. This was the time when they got together as a commune, spoke among themselves about themselves, their dreams and their problems. It was time for some peace and rest rather than work and boredom. Having a tube-well in their own tribal colony meant no more long walks with their friends. Their husbands now insisted that they fetch water from this well and this meant spending more time at their homes. This took away what they had been treasuring so much – their personal time, a shared space, privacy and the company of women whose lives and concerns they shared. In one loud voice they demanded an answer to why I had facilitated the provision of a tube well for their colony. They wanted to know how and why I had perceived that lack of water was their problem. They asked me why I did not have the patience or the need to ask them what they wanted.

I could see that they were right in what they were asking. What I saw as a problem was based on my perspective and background. I thought of a solution also from the same paradigm. I could only see the problem of water, of women walking long distances and the time they spent on all this. I was conditioned by the pressure of time that urban dwellers are used to and my spontaneous response was to see this as a problem of access to potable water and loss of 'productive' time. But they saw something else. For these women, these were not problems at all. Fetching water from such a long distance was never the problem. It was the lack of time for themselves, the inability of being with other women and sharing each other's life stories and dreams. The long walks provided the solution. Fetching water was the excuse; the real joy was in the walk, having a bath and washing their clothes on the riverbank and the leisurely walk back home. Once they returned, they knew that the drudgery of their domestic lives would resume.

Many a time, as development practitioners, we see the problem from the narrow lens of our own expertise and competence. It is like the famous saying: a man with a hammer will only see nails everywhere. We tend to see development as mere provision of education, health, livelihood, water and sanitation, etc. We limit our understanding to providing for man's basic physical needs without understanding the deeper requirements for the human heart, mind and soul. NGOs and governments alike have always prided themselves in ensuring the provision of basic amenities to the poor and marginalized. We tend to interpret problems of communities from the zone of our competence and strive to find solutions based on what we have and what we can do for them. And quite often, it has less to do with what people think they need and more to do with what we think they need. It is indeed convenient for us to restrict our understanding to this limited context as going deeper demands a lot more patience, humility and the ability to work as a partner with the people whom we are serving.

Development needs to be seen, interpreted and assessed not from the dimension of the agency, but from that of the community with whom we are working. We need to have the patience to listen, the time to reflect on what we have listened to and understood, and only then think of an intervention. There is a certain arrogance when we try to solve by ourselves, every problem that we encounter. At times, restraining ourselves from 'intervening' spontaneously can also be a good intervention. We need to guard ourselves from trying to impose 'our solution' and 'our views' on people. Only when we learn to respect the wisdom of people that we work with, only when we see them as equal partners and only when we empower them to solve their own problems will we be able to bring in 'development' that is democratic and meaningful. All else will only be notional and of no real significance.

"Will I get my firewood?" and other questions

This is an incident that goes back to the mid-nineties. An elderly woman, more than seventy years old at that time was among the many men and women of a forest based tribal community who were interacting with the Deputy Conservator of Forests (DCF), officer-in-charge of Nagarhole National Park[4]. These people were about to be displaced from their forests where they had been living for countless generations and their lives were about to be changed forever. The officer was making an attempt to understand the needs of this community, the major challenges they were likely to face and find ways of how the government could help them. Poshini[5], a lady who had spent several years working with these communities and had intimately known them was also present at the meeting upon the request of the Forest Department.

When she got a chance to speak, the elderly woman asked a simple question that surprised the officer and left him bemused. Poshini also felt disappointed and might have wondered about the impact of her efforts through the years to empower these communities.

4 Nagarhole National Park, also known as Rajiv Gandhi National Park is a protected natural reserve spread across Kodagu and Mysuru districts in the southern Indian state of Karnataka. The area was declared as a National Park in 1983 before which it was a wildlife sanctuary and further declared as a tiger reserve in 1999.

5 Poshini, an extremely committed lady to the cause of community empowerment, was the head of SVYM's Socio-economic Empowerment Program, a unit that focused on community development activities among the tribal communities of HD Kote Taluk in Mysuru district.

All that this elderly lady asked was whether she would continue to get her daily requirement of dry firewood if she moved and settled outside the National Park. Considering the situation where lives and livelihoods were poised to permanently change for scores of people, it seemed like an insignificant demand. But, years later as I reflect upon the incident, I realize that the elderly lady's question is pregnant with meaning and difficult to answer in more ways than one.

Mysuru in the southern Indian state of Karnataka is one of the districts that is home to a significant population of forest based tribes. There are five anthropologically distinct tribes who live in and around the Bandipur and Nagarhole forest ranges that skirt the district. For decades after India's independence, their lifestyles as well has livelihoods were traditionally enmeshed with what the forest offers as resources and often insulated from development as many of us see it. Things however started to change in the early sixties with the construction of a dam on the Kabini River that flows alongside Bandipur forest and with the passing of the Forest Conservation Act in 1972. Both these developments led to a massive upheaval in the lives of the tribal population in the region in terms of displacement, loss of livelihoods and cultural identities, and was accompanied by a rise of psycho-social and economic insecurity. It was the Forest Department's task to inform the people that they have to move out of the forest. The department also had to understand people's needs, and plan for compensation and resettlement.

This was the context of the DCF's interaction with this community. He, along with Subbaraya Kamath, one of the few humane and sensitive officers that I have known, were mulling the consequences of the displacement that was being planned by the Forest Department in Sunkadakatte forests located within the perimeter of the Nagarhole National Park. They had realized that conversations with the tribal community were in all likelihood going to be difficult and tense, and hence requested that they be accompanied by people from Swami Vivekananda Youth Movement. Poshini, who led the community development initiatives of the organization was the best suited person for this, not only because she was conversant with the issue, but also because she had a unique and one-to-one relationship with most of the tribal communities in the Taluk. Moreover, she was sensitive to their needs and aspirations and Poshini's presence was a way of ensuring that these communities found an empowered voice in these negotiations.

The manner in which the discussions took place gives us a good idea of the kind of efforts the government and its officials must put in getting something done on the ground meaningfully. This discussion started with the usual 'business like' approach that government officials are comfortable with. In a while, the tenor of the discussions became prescriptive, with the officials adopting the stance of 'benefactors', without an exploration or real understanding of what the community wanted. For anyone who has spent a reasonable amount of time living or working with these communities, it is easy to imagine the disconnect that would have prevailed in the atmosphere between what the officials were trying to say or offer, and the concerns and needs of the communities. Poshini also felt uneasy about the way these discussions were proceeding and intervened repeatedly to remind the officials that they were there to listen to the people rather than merely tell them what needed to be done. As a result, the mood and environment started turning slowly. The officials took their time in becoming comfortable with the idea of trying to understand what people were saying. Eventually, they realized the gulf between their perception of the problems, and the reality on the ground, and this was possible only because the officials involved were willing to see the other side and interpret carefully.

People's interpretation of poverty and their problems are often different from the conventional standpoint of the government and its enforcement machinery. The tribal communities did not interpret poverty as living with less than a dollar or two a day. Neither did they regard a government intervention that would help them augment their daily income as development. For a sensitive and curious person like Subbaraya Kamath, it was indeed a great lesson. But how many people in the system are sensitive enough to pick up these aspects or patient and humble enough to listen to these voices, let alone act on them? Can the system ever recognize that 'people' does not translate into a homogeneous mass, nor do their development aspirations?

The elderly tribal woman's question whether she will get her firewood every day is loaded with meaning and the answer is challenging in more ways than one. Besides, it leads to more pertinent questions. How could a government that only understands development in mere economic and measurable terms be able to interpret and deliver to this 'voiceless' citizen? How would development 'experts' be able to integrate social, cultural, political, and other basic rights into their frameworks?

Amartya Sen in his book 'Development as Freedom' talks about people being able to expand the freedoms we have reason to value. And in understanding this value, lies the true relevance of any development intervention. How will anyone understand that 'development' goes beyond looking at mere utilitarian and libertarian issues? What place will 'personal freedom' and 'choice' have in the various schemes that the government's planners conceive of? Will the voice of wisdom from this inconspicuous tribal hamlet in a geographically challenged setting find a place in the way the government thinks of displacement and development? How can anyone amortize and measure the 'value' of dry firewood being available each day for this tribal woman whose life revolves around the forest and what it provides? Can these concepts of what is of value to people, their freedom and choice be recognized and factored in the different development programs that governmental as well as non-governmental agencies design and implement?

There are several other questions, but what is crucial is that policy makers and development practitioners truly make an attempt to ask them, reflect on them and answer them. It may not be possible for them to find all the answers by themselves and that is exactly why people must be involved in the process, at each stage, to make 'development' relevant.

Development with dignity

Jadiya belongs to the Jenukuruba tribal community, who lived not far from Hosahalli, a place where a residential school exclusively for forest based tribal children of Heggadadevanakote Taluk of Mysuru district has been established and presently provides education to more than four hundred children every year. Back in 1988, it was a small set-up with just twenty eight students and run by a small but extremely committed group of people. We had just managed to fence some five acres of land given to us for the campus by the government and wanted to take advantage of an extended monsoon that year. We decided that we would plant trees in the campus all along the fence and procured around two thousand saplings of various kinds from the forest department. Thanks to the extraordinary enthusiasm, energy and efforts of the students, we managed to clear the campus of the shrubs, and stockpile all of it so that it served as fuel for the school kitchen for the next three to four months. Apart from that, there were also small pits dug up by the students to plant the saplings. In about a month's time all the saplings were planted during which, Marikala, the man who led this entire exercise on the ground, would take me around the campus every evening and proudly show me the fruits of the day's work.

However, there was one little spanner thrown in the tenacious works of Marikala and the children. An enterprising goat managed to sneak into the campus every day and make some of the plants its breakfast or lunch. This went on for some time and one day Marikala was finally able to nab the culprit and tie it up by going out early to the campus. The idea was to wait for its owner and soon enough, Jadiya, who lived nearby strolled into the campus looking for his goat. He saw the goat tied up and asked us to release it. We explained to Jadiya that the efforts and aspirations of the children were being chewed away by his goat and that he must do something about it.

Jadiya became defensive and tried to tell us that we should protect our plants better, though he was well aware of the challenges of putting in place someone to man the remote campus. He even offered to sell his goat to us, if it were so much of a problem. The arguments heated up and no reasonable or amicable solution seemed visible. In the heat of the moment, I lost control and retorted angrily. I told him that the food his family had been consuming for the past month was given by us, and that some clothes given to his family were part of somebody's donation. For a moment, there was silence. I did not realize the implication of what I had said at that time. Jadiya spoke nothing and turned away in disgust. Marikala and I stood there, watching.

Jadiya returned in a while and threw a saree in my face. He said that the *ragi* (finger millet, a staple food of the communities in the region) he had received could not be returned because they had consumed it, but he could still ask his wife to give the saree. What he spoke further is a lesson in development that none of us should forget, especially if we identify ourselves as development practitioners, workers or advocates. Jadiya told me that his family had survived even before we came there and can continue to do so even in our absence. Poverty meant nothing to him. He told me that he may be poor in an economic sense, but he and his community were rich in their sense of dignity and self-esteem. He said he accepted the *ragi* and saree not with the feeling of a beggar, but like receiving a gift from a friend and brother. Even this argument and this fight, he told me, was in this spirit. But now things were different because he felt that he was only a beggar in my view. He could no longer keep the saree with himself, nor could he engage with me again, with the same feelings as before.

The entire episode offers a great lesson for development interventionists. Working with communities with a feeling of sympathy and a paternalistic attitude can lead to disempowerment rather than empowerment, and we must guard against it. Whether it is led by NGOs, governments or companies by way of their social responsibility initiatives, no activity can yield meaningful results unless it is undertaken with a spirit of partnership and mutual respect. Else, it is just an ego-gratifying exercise.

This is not to say that people must not receive benefits of interventions and programs, and that the communities who receive them are undeserving of them. The benefits and provisions of programs would only have deeper significance if they are viewed as a way of co-empowering people, rather than being given out as doles for personal or political gains. Almost all political parties in the recent past have indulged in theatrics where billions of rupees worth of goods and services are distributed to 'beneficiaries'.

In March 2012, more than 110,000 families in Mysuru district were handed out various benefits under different schemes by the Chief Minister of the state. The event was named *Sarkari Savalattu Santhe*, translating to a market of provisions being made available by the government. It was truly a market, wherein different products were being made available to people. The only difference is that one could not necessarily get what one really wanted, but would have to take what a patronizing government was willing to give. Whether or not the government had really understood the needs of the people is a moot point. Arguably, the onus is on government to make sure that the poorest of the poor do not lose out on the benefits of the measures undertaken, and its intent to reach out to a large number of people quickly is appreciable. But events that are intended to achieve narrow political gains make the poor vulnerable and rob them of their dignity and self-respect, while also taking away the human spirit of enterprise. Even the most ardent proponents of welfare economics would agree that it is detrimental in the long run.

Measuring development

When I first came to the forests of Heggadadevanakote in Mysuru district of South India in the 1980s, I began running a small dispensary with the intention of serving the indigenous population of that area. Medicine was all that I had learned and my focus, along with those who supported the initiative at that time, was on providing medical care. Obstetrics was one of my favorite subjects, and it was only natural that I paid greater attention to maternal health and mortality. Public health knowledge and practice of the time had established maternal mortality to be an important indicator of the health of a community. It was also the time when everyone, including the WHO and Government of India, focused heavily on maternal health and safe motherhood initiatives. The entire health sector was pushing the practice of institutional deliveries and we also got caught up in this excitement.

Being concerned about the high maternal mortality in the area, we started exploring how it could be brought down. Over the next many years, we campaigned for institutional deliveries and ensured that we created adequate facilities for safe childbirth at our hospitals. SVYM implemented a World Bank funded project in 2001-02 to ensure improved maternal and child health outcomes amongst the tribals in the area. In addition to providing facilities, there were massive efforts taken towards influencing behavioral changes among the communities and getting the women to opt for institutional deliveries.

My wife Bindu, an obstetrician who was associated with the program remarked one day that she was seeing a huge positive change with regard to the healthcare-seeking behavior of tribal women. She told me how challenging it was twenty five years back, to motivate the tribal women towards opting institutional deliveries, but now the women sought the hospital on their own. Institutional deliveries were non-existent when I first came to the area. By the end of the World Bank funded project in 2002, institutional deliveries had grown to 40%. Today, virtually every tribal woman in the area comes to our hospitals to deliver her baby. Our Reproductive and Child Health (RCH) programs have been written about and studied; the World Bank considered the RCH project they funded us, as one of their best, and public health practitioners and academicians were impressed with the falling maternal mortality and improved health outcomes. It was indeed very reassuring when so many people and institutions with their sophisticated tools and methods called our endeavor a public health success. It could be construed that we had contributed significantly to development in that area, at least with regard to maternal health.

This begets the question: how can we really measure 'development'? In an age where we are obsessed with measuring everything in definitive terms, be it our wealth, our academic success, a movie or play that we have seen, or the experience of service in a flight or a hotel, we tend to measure and rate everything that we do, without perhaps pausing to think why are we measuring something and what metrics are being used. 'What cannot be measured, cannot be managed' is also a mantra espoused by the management and strategy world, and with good reasons. In the 'development' sector, which is dependent on grant making agencies and donors, and where academics are playing an ever-increasing role, the obsession of measuring and evaluating programs, outcomes and outputs is at an unprecedented high. Entire programs and the underlying efforts can be deemed a failure or success based on the parameters to measure them, and people's competence to truly comprehend the metrics, the tools and context.

Using the metrics of improved health outcomes and the falling maternal mortality and morbidity rates, our program was undoubtedly a success. But were these the right metrics to measure our work and intent? Could these metrics capture everything that existed in this ecosystem? Would it be honest on our part if we did not engage with the unintentional outcomes of our programs, which may have not been given enough attention or considered not worthy of measurement at the time the programs were launched? Can we choose to remain ignorant of the metrics that one needed to deploy to measure these outcomes? And if we make it our primary goal to meet the targets defined by the metrics, can we ever claim to have a holistic approach towards development in our programs?

Certain metrics also serve to hide some of the unintended effects of development interventions. In our attempt to reduce maternal mortality by increasing institutional deliveries, had we not unintentionally taken away the community's ability to cope and manage this natural phenomenon without any dependence on people or a system outside their community and tradition? Today, we have a generation of young women who have mostly delivered their babies in our hospitals, but who have neither the knowledge, the attitude nor experience to ensure that they can continue their centuries' old tradition of delivering children at home, or even be prepared to handle any contingency situation, if faced with one. We are left questioning the validity of metrics as well as the tools, however refined they might have been.

Somewhere, we must also have the courage and innovation to turn the metrics on their head. What, if we had changed the metric to building the capacity and competence of the community to have cost-effective and rational health practices that did not need an expensive health care system. Isn't building the capacity and competence of communities to ensure a workable health system that they can run and sustain with their own resources and abilities more important than running a sophisticated health care program that needs doctors, nurses and managers to come from faraway cities?

The development sector needs to focus on arriving at metrics to measure what is important for communities, rather than sticking to what is easily measurable, such as programmatic and managerial aspects of interventions. Further, the metrics ought to be able to capture what is happening in the whole ecosystem rather than the piece that is most evident. What is needed is a fair representation of the growth of human and social capital that accompanies the implementation of any project.

We need to capture how the capabilities of the people and communities involved in the development process expand or shrink due to the intervention that is deployed. We need metrics to capture not only the empowerment processes but also the growth in cognitive, social and emotional skills of the people engaged in the entire process. We need metrics to capture interdependence, reciprocity and trust amongst the many players involved, which would help reveal the expansion of social capital as a result of the interventions. We also need to pay attention to the inherent and existing capacities of the people and traditional societies in being able to institutionalize change and socio-economic mobility. There is indeed tremendous scope for innovation and emergence of tools and methodologies to measure those aspects of development that truly matter.

It is also critical to build citizen-centric, partnership-based and community-led processes into program evaluations, so that the emerging psycho-social, political and economic changes can be effectively assessed. While more and more complex and sophis-ticated tools to prove correlations and causality like randomized control trials are being introduced to the development sector, one must be aware and cautious, and see to it that they do not further alienate people working at the grassroots and communities. Smaller community based organizations neither have the resources nor the bandwidth to develop the skills needed to deploy these tools. The need of the hour is to develop socially relevant tools that people at the grassroots level can be involved in and deploy, but also understand and interpret. Unless this happens, people's participation will remain notional and development will continue to be driven by so called 'domain experts' and will further promote the already existing information and power asymmetries.

Innovation in the development sector

A few years ago, 'innovation' seemed to be the buzzword going around. In early 2011, the Karnataka Knowledge Commission had invited me to a meeting for the formation of the State Innovation Council. At around the same time, the Tata group, one of India's largest business conglomerates had invited me to speak at 'Innovista' – a meeting of all their companies in the southern region to celebrate the successes of their innovations and reflect upon the failures. I was also invited by the Karnataka Chapter of the Confederation of Indian Industry to present my views at an event in Bengaluru where 'India', 75 years after its independence, was being envisioned. Innovation was the common theme in all these events.

Innovation indeed is a crucial part of the development vision, whether it is of the state or of private agencies. However, what left me concerned from my experience at these events was that the discourse on innovation, for most of the stakeholders involved, was confined to industry and technology. Somehow, the concept of innovation was relegated to breakthroughs in products and services. I was surprised that hardly any of them had thought that one could innovate in the social sector.

Innovation comes from the Latin root 'Innovatinem' which means 'to renew' or 'to change' and the usage of the word came into existence in 1540. In a very basic way, it is a term used to describe a process that renews something that exists. It could be a change in thought process or could refer to a process of change that is incremental, radical or emergent. In the last few decades, innovation has been used with a strong correlation to economic growth in development, especially since the time of Joseph Schumpeter's popular book 'Capitalism, Socialism and Democracy' written in 1942. The *Economist* defines innovation as "new products, business processes or organic changes that create wealth or social welfare" or simply "the fresh thinking that creates value". But, as long as value is measured in economic terms, the meaning and scope of 'innovation' will remain limited to a narrow understanding. Such innovation tends to be a closed process, relying on a limited pool of human resources and knowledge, especially that of the 'experts', and is largely driven by companies, individual innovators or specialized designers rather than by those who are ultimate users of the innovations, or communities at large.

Innovation indeed is a major driving force in global economic growth and development, but can we limit ourselves to this narrow understanding of the term? If innovation is to be one of the drivers of India's growth, wouldn't it be immeasurably significant to look at innovation from the context of social and economic justice in the country? Could innovation in the social sector be something that can provide answers to our numerous problems? Could it help us in reducing the enormous inequities that have become increasingly visible with unprecedented economic growth? What could innovation mean in the context of the growing conflicts and the changing role of the state, civil society and the private sector? Should economic growth be the primary driver of innovation for the social sector too? Shouldn't there be scope for innovation in addressing the social and environmental problems arising out of high economic growth? These are critical questions that one needs to reflect upon, especially if one is working at the grassroots level where the direct impact of innovations or the lack of it, is visible and palpable.

It is pertinent to understand what factors influence innovation in a particular sector or sphere of activities. Innovation in the private sector is driven by competitiveness, profitability and the desire to reduce costs constantly. It may be argued that these are factors that limit the perimeter of innovation, but a quick look at the public or the government sector shows that these are the very factors that are missing in them. NGOs on the other hand may be driven both by passion to bring positive changes as well as the need to keep costs low, so that their interventions are sustainable, but are often constrained by human, technical and financial resources.

In the Indian context, the government has a virtual monopoly on ensuring social growth and therefore little reason to be innovative. The little space that NGOs had created for themselves has been surrendered to the government due to changes in policies and dependency on the government for financial support. The only innovation that the government is now talking about is to move from being a direct provider of services to provisioning them through NGOs. This in fact takes away the innovativeness of NGOs as they are reduced to being mere contractors and are forced to fall in line with government policies and dictums.

Governments, by the very nature of their structure and function have no space for 'profitability'. In fact, in the Indian context, this could very well be a negative driver of the government, especially keeping in mind the various political compulsions under which they operate. It is ironical that the government in the early 1960s and 70s started numerous industrial undertakings that today are models of inefficient and corrupt administrations. They seem to exist more to pay salaries to their employees and serve as instruments to confer favors by the political class on their followers.

Many years ago, when Rajiv Gandhi was the Prime Minister of India, he had lamented in the Parliament that out of every hundred rupees spent on development by the government, only fifteen rupees reached the people for whom it was meant. The Performance Evaluation Organization of the Planning Commission of India estimated that the government spends Rs. 13.31 per kg on unintended subsidies to give an intended subsidy of Rs. 5.46 per kg of food grains for the poor in the Public Distribution System. The state of affairs extends to the entire spectrum of public services and the government's welfare measures. There is a crying need for innovativeness in addressing inefficiency and governance-deficits in public services. In fact, it is needed to tackle the innovativeness with which the system is compromised through pilferage and corruption at all scales.

Innovation is indeed needed in the onerous task of delivering goods and services to the millions of our marginalized and socio-economically weaker sections of the population, who need a safety net to get out of the trap of poverty. Just imagine how much our government could do and achieve if only it were to become more competitive and cost effective, and was driven by efficient processes and systems. A more responsive and inclusive system can not only deliver outcomes that result in better human development, but also serve to reduce the ever-widening gap of inequity significantly.

But can this happen in isolation? Will a government machinery habituated to decades of inefficient administrative practices, and with huge stakes in inefficiency, be driven to change its attitude and functioning? In my own opinion, only an enlightened citizenry and an active civil society can drive the government to undertake this metamorphosis. By itself, the incentives to not perform are too lucrative to think of change. One way of addressing the issue and moving forward is to relook at the scope of Public-Private Partnerships (PPP) and take it beyond areas such as creating infrastructure and profit-making ventures like building ports, airports and toll roads. While the passion and progressive thinking that civil society harbors must be factored in, the private sector must also become socially conscious and share skills, competencies and knowledge with the public sector to render it more efficient.

This is not an argument that the government should move away from providing the basic services that are targeted at social and economic upliftment of people. What is needed is the introduction of dimensions of greater efficiency and accountability. It is totally unacceptable that while companies have world-class logistics management systems and practices, which ensure that goods reach the shelves of their retail outlets hundreds and thousands of kilometers away, some government departments still maintain their inventory manually. With the resources available at the government's disposal, it should ideally outperform the private sector.

Innovation towards better delivery of public services, innovations to address the last mile issues and innovations in access to programs, schemes and information that leave communities empowered must be collectively worked on. These innovations would essentially combine people's participation, technology, good governance and information sharing as part of the solutions. In fact, there are examples to demonstrate that this combination works successfully. GRAAM's initiative of empowering community representatives to monitor the facilities and services of their Primary Health Centers (PHCs) using technology, effectively illustrates an innovation in the social sector that results in improvement of services as well as relationships between the community and health functionaries at the grassroots.

Titled Arogyashreni[6], the project allowed community representatives from rural Mysuru to answer an automated voice-based questionnaire related to facilities and services in their government run Primary Health Centers over their mobile phones. Their answers were recorded in a server and analyzed to get information about the health centers across the district and also to rank them. This process further inspired the community representatives to deliberate on the issues and advocate for local solutions as well. The experience shows that communities are willing to be part of innovative processes that results in local changes in the way they envisage.

6 Explained in greater detail in the article 'Making advocacy a community movement' pp 264

Engaging communities in their own development is an area that provides ample scope for innovativeness. Statutory processes such as social audits of works and entitlements under Mahatma Gandhi National Rural Employment Guarantee Act are innovative ideas that must be rigorously implemented. Use of technology that makes the Right to Information Act even more effective in breaking the asymmetry of information, and thereby power are being attempted in states like Bihar and must be strongly promoted.

Land usage is another area that demands innovation in how rewards of growth can be distributed equitably. I am neither a votary of mindless industrialization nor an opponent of justified and viable industrial growth. Nevertheless, in those instances where farmers and indigenous communities are inevitably displaced, it remains to be sincerely explored whether the original inhabitants of the land can be made shareholders and receive dividends. Innovations that keep the best interest of the ordinary citizens as the focal point can not only reduce unrest, as seen in dozens of cases in India, but also ensure people's socio-economic growth.

Innovation for socio-economic growth requires genuine interest and commitment, towards equity, fairness and pursuit of local development. The Taluk of Heggadadevanakote in Mysuru district is home to three rivers, four reservoirs and three power plants. The plants produce 27 megawatts of power among them. The peak load demand of the entire Taluk is around 5 megawatt, but the Taluk ends up getting only 1.5 megawatt and the remaining goes to the rest of the state through the main grid. Simple ways of ensuring local distribution of power through micro-grids could have helped the Taluk reap the benefits of power that the Taluk generates itself. Why is it that local development suffers, especially of those areas that are rich in natural resources, despite providing these very resources for development elsewhere? In this case, it is pertinent to note that Heggadadevanakote ranks among the most backward Taluks of the state.

Innovation is all about looking into the future and responding to the demands that one can anticipate. Innovating for the social sector needs public agencies to fine-tune the art of listening to communities and building their own capacities to respond to their aspirations. While technology and cutting edge innovation processes can increase the scale and efficiency with which social problems affecting the poor and vulnerable sections of our population are addressed, we must realize that innovation does not always mean breakthroughs in complex situations. Simplification is also an innovation, and of high importance, especially in the social sector. Public and service delivery institutions need to recognize the power of innovation processes to further their work and employ them to improve their organizational strategy and programmatic performance, which shall pave way for development that truly matters.

"THE ONLY TYRANT I ACCEPT IN THIS
WORLD IS THE 'STILL SMALL VOICE'
WITHIN ME. AND EVEN THOUGH I
HAVE TO FACE THE PROSPECT OF
BEING A MINORITY OF ONE, I HUMBLY
BELIEVE I HAVE THE COURAGE TO BE
IN SUCH A HOPELESS MINORITY."

MAHATMA GANDHI

Voices from the grassroots level

In the discourse on development, it is the powerful and the elite who often hold sway. This is a matter of concern. Even more worrying is their simplistic view of issues faced by rural, tribal or socio-economically weaker communities, and their instant assessment of the problem as well as its solution. I am no stranger to this phenomenon myself as I had held similar thoughts in my initial years of living and working among the tribal communities. Experience taught me, sometimes the hard way, that understanding grassroots perspectives takes more than a few conversations with people. It involves listening deeply and with humility as well as an ability to learn and appreciate the other's views; patience to reflect, and perseverance to interpret things carefully.

I have been fortunate through my life and career to have the opportunity to listen to people in varied settings, understand issues from their perspective and reflect upon what 'development' means to them. I have the conviction to say that without listening to the voices emanating from the grassroots, no meaningful development can ever happen. In this section, I have tried to capture those voices, the wisdom contained in them, lessons for us, and more importantly questions whose simplicity belies the complexity of finding answers to them. The task for policy makers and policy advocates is to incorporate these voices in the development initiatives they conceive and implement.

An identity for Akkamma

Akkamma sounded agitated on the phone. She wanted to know why she had to go through the process of being identified and declared as 'Akkamma' at a place remote from her village and by someone who didn't know her at all. She had evidently never faced a situation where she had to prove who she was. It took a while for Poshini, who had received her call, to calm her down and understand the problem.

Akkamma belongs to the Jenukuruba[7] community from Bavikere tribal colony and has been an active member of the women's self-help group, the initiation of which was facilitated by SVYM. She, and the fellow members of her group had been made aware of the government's programs towards ensuring food security, especially the Public Distribution System (PDS) and its provisions. She knew that she belonged to a category of beneficiaries under the PDS, who were eligible to get an Antyodaya card[8], which entitled her family to receive twenty nine kilograms of highly subsidized food grains each month from the local Fair Price Shop.

However, knowing what she was eligible for wasn't enough to claim her entitlements. It wasn't even enough if the persons

7 Jenukurubas are one of the Particularly Vulnerable Tribal Groups (PVTG) who reside in the southern districts of Karnataka whose traditional occupation is honey-gathering from the forests.

8 Cards issued by the Department of Food, Civil Supplies and Consumer Affairs to extremely poor families that entitles them to receive maximum benefits from the Public Distribution System.

operating the local Fair Price Shop knew her and what she was eligible for, without the necessary documentation. Akkamma spent more than sixty rupees to go to Heggadadevanakote, the Taluk headquarters, where the documents were to be processed. On meeting the concerned officials, she was told that she had to produce an affidavit establishing her identity as Akkamma from Bavikere village. The request felt quite strange to her. She neither understood what this meant nor how someone in this town more than thirty kilometers from her village could confirm her identity. She was further told that a notary could certify and give an affidavit to this effect.

Akkamma was thoroughly confused. In her own simplistic way, she had called up Poshini wanting to know why someone from her village or nearby was not entitled to do this and how could someone not known to her at all prove and establish her identity. Akkamma's question was indeed profound. All that she wanted to know was how the government could trust an 'affidavit' purchased for a hundred rupees or so and not take her word that she was indeed the person she claimed to be. She wanted to know how her identity was not based on who she was but on the word of someone who was paid to tell who she was.

Akkamma's query would surely find resonance in thousands of poor, illiterate, but profoundly intelligent indigenous women like her. It is an innocent query that hides many deeper questions beneath it. Can one's identity be established at a price? Is there a price for citizenship? What does 'entitlement' truly mean? And where does the sense of identity flow from? Our own sense of 'self' or from what the government through its agents and processes determine us to be?

These questions mean a lot to the majority of India's population, which lives below some line or the other: of poverty, social hierarchy, educational levels, health and nutritional status, and consequently deprived of the 'fruits of development'. Though numerous programs and schemes are floated by the government with the noble intention of uplifting the population socially and economically, they fall short of their desired goal by not reaching the intended beneficiaries. Looking at the kind of budgets allocated for flagship programs such as the health mission, universal education, public distribution of subsidized food grains or the rural employment guarantee scheme, it is natural to desire accuracy in identifying beneficiaries. In a country whose population exceeds a billion, the process is indeed challenging, but when a truly inclusive approach is adopted, I wonder if identifying the deserving poor is really as complex as it is made out to be.

The government, on the other hand, seems to have a ready-made answer to the problem of identification in the form of *Aadhaar*, an initiative to provide citizens with a unique 12-digit identification number combined with the capture of biometric information of the individual. The notion that schemes will be better implemented because of *Aadhaar* is at best illusory since it is based on an incorrect premise that pilferage, exclusion and misappropriation of resources under various government schemes is attributed to poor identification. It is collusion and fraud at the middle and higher levels of the system that largely incapacitate the delivery mechanisms of programs and not the people living in underserved areas.

Yet, people like Akkamma have to go through convoluted procedures of identification evolved by the state before it provides services to its citizenry. The state fails to understand that her identity is centered on her transactions with her community and interdependence on people who matter in her life and livelihood, which includes the local service providers. It is also based on trust and an intimate knowledge of her social and economic status among the people around her. No centrally controlled mechanism can establish a more accurate identity for Akkamma than what can be done locally. The onus of guaranteeing inclusion also lies as much on the local community and governance structure as the government. The real question is whether the government trusts Akkamma and millions like her, and their identities. Isn't the 'trust' that the government ought to have in people like Akkamma also an 'entitlement'? Is there an answer in collective citizen action that can find answers to Akkamma's questions? Can we help find an identity for Akkamma, the citizen?

Leadership lessons from Kempaiah

Leadership is indeed a much used and abused term. In a workshop on leadership that I was conducting, I recollect asking participants how many of them wanted to be a leader and how many wanted to be managers. Every one of them, without an exception wanted to be a leader. Each one of us have our own interpretation of leadership and there are thousands of books on leadership written and published around the world every year.

I have always believed that leadership is innate to every individual and one only needs to manifest it appropriately. One has to call upon one's inner resources and respond to each situation adaptively to function as a leader. In my view, leadership is not a decoration or even a position, but an ability to summon and mobilize resources both within and around us to achieve a common constructive goal together amidst enormous uncertainty. Having lived amongst the indigenous tribal communities for more than two decades, I have witnessed the manifestation of some of the finest leadership qualities among tribal chieftains. Called *Yajamana* within their communities, they command respect and loyalty from their folk, but their ability to face tumultuous times and hardships are often hidden.

This is the story of Kempaiah, a *Yajamana* of the Kadukuruba tribe. He and his people were forcibly relocated in 1972 by the forest department from the Bandipur forests as a result of the introduction of the Forest Conservation Act, which considered human activity in the forests to be detrimental to the conservation process. Having lost their home and hearth, they settled themselves on the fringes of their beloved forests and their hamlet was named as 'Kempanahadi' (the hamlet of Kempaiah). When I first met him in 1987, Kempaiah was around sixty five years of age and had his long gray hair tied into a bun. He carried a small bag around his neck containing betel-nuts and one always found him chewing on them incessantly. Kempaiah loved to talk and would come to meet me every other day.

Our discussions many a time turned to the lives of the tribal people in the forest. There were stories of how the communities lived, their dependence on whatever the forest offered them and the fact that they never felt deprived. There were conversations about how life was different before the communities were asked to relocate from what was a home to them for generations. On one such occasion, the conversation centered on the emotional pain that relocation left. It would have been no surprise if there was anguish and disappointment in Kempaiah's narrative. Instead, he narrated the incident of his community being forcibly moved out of the forest in a very matter-of-fact manner. He neither had any anger nor hatred towards the department that had caused such deep anguish for him and his people. Their lives and lifestyles of thousands of years had changed permanently, yet there was no bitterness in his voice.

I found his attitude strange and inferred that it was born out of helplessness and asked him how he could stay unmoved by all that had happened. Kempaiah's explanations left me speechless. He told me that though emotions had their own role in leading his people, he had to take care that he did not get carried away by them. He had to ensure that emotions did not cloud his judgment and he had to accept what came his way. As the *Yajamana* or the leader of his people, he felt that it was his duty to stay grounded, maintain poise and not lose focus. Getting emotional would not only cloud his judgment, but would also possibly prevent him from arriving at the right decisions.

He explained to me that life in the forests had taught him to live in the present and not really worry about the future. The entire tribal culture and lifestyle revolved around living in the present and he lamented that moving out of the forest would have consequences deeper than what one could imagine. He added that his greater concern was that his people would lose their way and move away from living in the present to worrying about their future and romantically dream about how they lived in the past. He considered losing the tribal interpretation of life, which contains a certain sense of equanimity, as a bigger danger than the loss of their forests and land. He had to make sure that his people saw that and had to guard his people against losing what was of greater value.

Looking back now, I can see the extraordinary visionary that Kempaiah was. I can now explain his serene look and infectious humor. I have now begun to understand that it is not the events themselves, but our own reactions and interpretations of these events that shape our leadership abilities. Kempaiah was not one who had become a *Yajamana* just by an accident of tradition. He was a true leader, who in his own way had understood what self-awareness was and how critical it was in leading people under such difficult circumstances.

Kempaiah is no more and I miss his loud laughter and *paan*[9]-spewing conversations. More than anything, the world will miss his brand of enlightened leadership that it needs so badly today. Kempaiah's lessons were not limited to leadership alone. The value of selfless work, trusting each other and the wisdom to live in the present were lessons that not only Kempaiah, but many other indigenous friends constantly continue to illustrate in the way they live and approach the world. In comparison, there is much ground that modern civilization has to cover in terms of learning to live.

9 Betel leaf rolled or folded over a filling of areca nut and other ingredients including tobacco at times and chewed

Learning from first generation school-goers

The school, located in Hosahalli that today educates more than four hundred forest-based tribal children every year had its beginnings in a makeshift arrangement in a cowshed in a hamlet named Brahmagiri in 1988. The first batch of the 'school' had twenty eight children and the experience of running a school and interacting with the children and their communities had more lessons than any textbook could provide. None of us who started the school had any notable semblance of a background or experience in the education sector. We started a center for learning nevertheless, on the back of unbridled enthusiasm and goodwill of the communities.

Back then, we had to make our own arrangements for the mid-day meal amidst the 'classes' or academic sessions. Cooking and having lunch at the school was great fun with responsibilities being shared between children and adults alike. A few of us would decide on the menu, which unfailingly was *ragi* (finger-millet) balls and *sambar*[10] every day. A few more would collect the firewood required to light up our hearth of three stones, while some others would cut the few vegetables that we could lay our hands on. A few children would then mold cooked *ragi* flour into small balls called *mudde*. Some others would take on the responsibility of serving their friends and a couple of them had to clean up after the whole

---

10 Sambar, a common South Indian dish is a lentil based soupy preparation flavored with Indian spices and consumed with rice usually by pouring over it.

thing was done. All this took more time than the academic work, but that was what the fun was all about.

One day, it was the turn of seven-year old Manju to make the *ragi* balls. That day he had brought along with him, his kid sister Sunanda to school. The first thought that crossed my mind on seeing her was, "Oh my God! Another mouth to feed today!" I expected Manju to roll an extra ball for her and was quite surprised when I saw him make only twenty eight. This aroused my curiosity and I started watching him keenly. All twenty eight plates were laid out and I saw him seat his sister next to him. Surely but slowly, he broke his *ragi* ball into two and shared it with his sister. I could not contain my curiosity and took Manju aside after the meal and asked him the question that I was bursting with: why did he not make the twenty ninth ball for his sister? He gave a reply that still resonates in my ears.

With all his innocence, this tribal child gave me an insight into the value system that these simple, yet refined people possessed. He told me that his parents had gone to the local shandy, a weekly market, to sell their bamboo ware. While he wanted to make sure his sister was taken care of, he also did not want to miss school. And though it was his responsibility to feed her, he did not want his classmates to share his burden. So, it was natural for him to share his meal with his little sister.

I was moved to tears as I tried to reflect on the great wisdom coming from this young child. I realized how this school was indeed educating me by getting me to unlearn all the selfishness that I had grown up with and making me understand that I needed to take responsibility for my actions and not transfer the burden onto society, my family and friends. It was helping me understand that there was a teacher in each person I met and in every event that took place around me. While Manju was trying to figure out what he had said that upset me so much, his own actions were nothing out of the ordinary for him. It was just another day and that was the way he lived. His values came from his people, his culture, and his family who lived in harmony with nature and the forests and respectfully accepted whatever there was on offer.

Despite acknowledging that values constitute a greater part of education than the lessons contained in textbooks, I wonder if we can ever expect our school to impart the values and knowledge that these tribal children already seem to possess. The school does provide a platform for the children to acquire skills that would help them integrate with mainstream society and make use of opportunities that the world out there has in store, but it should certainly not be at the cost of making them unlearn what they already know. It is indeed a fine balance and a difficult one to strike: on the one hand we constantly come across instances where the tribal people have been short-changed because of their innocence, and on the other, there is a struggle to retain a certain identity and the accompanying values, ethos and their natural knowledge.

Another incident from our early days with the school throws light on the vast knowledge that is natural to even the children of indigenous communities. The government had allocated land for our school in 1987, but we were yet to have a building to run the school in. For nearly a year, we conducted our classes in the open. One day, we were all working together to clear the shrubs and make some space for our dream called 'school'. Everyone including the children, was toiling away and after a while, the children were getting tired and bored. So, we decided to take a break and have some fun. I had to hurriedly think of something interesting and I suggested that each child try and count the trees that we had on our campus. Someone suggested that they would not only count the trees, but also get a leaf from each tree. Then someone else added that they needed to do all this within an hour. Off they went, in different directions and an hour or so later, they started trickling in with a huge bunch of leaves. Each child started counting the leaves – most had around thirty, some had fifty, but what Manju had brought surprised me. He had leaves from nearly seventy different trees. So many different shapes and sizes, though many looked alike to me. He not only counted them out, but as he did so, explained to me which tree would shed its leaf first, which tree would attract the most bees and how drinking honey from the '*Taare*[11]' tree would cause temporary insanity!

And here I was, thinking that these children needed schooling! I could not have been more wrong. Our organization may have started a school for communities who have never gone to school before, but the lessons they have taught us, and the indigenous knowledge, values and philosophy that we witness so often, fill us with humility. The least we ought to ensure is to not let schooling interfere with their inherent education.

---

11 *Taare* (Terminalia bellirica) tree is a large deciduous tree native to the Western Ghats of India

The spirit of partnership

Of the many extraordinary people I have met in my life and have been supported by, Thimmiah stands apart for the kind of values he lived by and the kind of lessons I have learned from him. I had first met Thimmiah, a Jenukuruba tribal in 1987 when our organization had been allotted five acres of land in a remote hamlet called Hosahalli to build a school exclusively for children of forest based tribes. When we were looking for somebody to watch over the land before the school was built, I found that Thimmiah out of his own conviction had taken it upon himself to safeguard the land as a way of making his contribution to the school. And for years, Thimmiah, the self-appointed custodian of the land continued to look after it and was around, offering his wit and wisdom even after the school was well established with nearly four hundred children milling around the campus. Without selfless people like him, I wonder if we could have ever achieved all that we have.

In recognition of Thimmiah's contributions, arrangements had been made to ensure that he and his family always received adequate meals from the school's kitchen. Apart from this, we arranged for the government to allot to him, a patch of land measuring around an acre and a half in area, which he and his wife had converted through hard work, into an orchard with many fruit-bearing trees like lemon, guava, mango and jackfruit. He had started a ritual of giving me the first fruits harvested every season, and even after I had moved out of Hosahalli, he would somehow ensure that the fruits reached me. I felt that this was his way of thanking me for all that had been provided.

Over time, age and disease had caught up with Thimmiah and despite my constant chiding, he had not given up smoking and had contracted tuberculosis too. He was very poor in his compliance with the treatment and would take his medicines whenever he felt like it. The personnel at the hospital and the outreach workers were getting increasingly frustrated with him. Every time he slipped on his medications, they would complain to me and ask me to use my 'influence' over him and coax or reprimand him into being more compliant. Some days he would relent, on most other days he wouldn't.

It was one such day and I was also nearing the end of my patience. I met Thimmiah and tried to reason with him, patiently explaining what his non-compliance would cost him and his community. I felt irritated and let down that no amount of reasoning was working and our discussion was going nowhere. I made no headway either as a friend or as a physician. Then I snapped. I lost my cool and blurted out that he needed to show me some regard and even gratitude for the land, the saplings and all the other forms of 'help' that I had given him and his family over the years. It was something I wish I had never uttered. There was silence for a while before Thimmiah responded, a response that is still fresh in my memory.

He seemed unaffected and calmly mentioned to me that he was indeed sorry that he had received all the 'help' that was given. He said he was confused now, as he had always felt that I was not a 'provider' but a partner in his progress. He remarked that he never saw the 'other' in me and felt that we were working together in creating something wonderful. The garden neither belonged to me nor to him. I could claim no ownership because I facilitated getting the land and saplings while he could also not make any claims just because the land ownership documents were in his name or because he toiled day and night on the land. He explained that the land and the fruits belonged to both of us as much as it did to the whole world. His ritual of giving me the fruits each year was not his way of thanking me, but his way of reminding me not to make him feel obliged to me and to send out the message of partnership. He wanted to communicate in his own wise way that we were not obliged to each other, but should actually feel obliged to nature and the circumstances that gave us this extraordinary opportunity of working together. He felt that I needed to see my act of helping him get the land and the saplings as the beginning of a partnership where his part of the deal was to till and tend to the plants and the garden. In this partnership, he reasoned that our dignity would not only be maintained but also grow. In making one of us the 'provider' and the other the 'receiver', we were reducing this extraordinary development process to a very narrow interpretation of charity.

I was astounded at his explanation and was trying to process all that he was saying. His explanation was simplistic and yet so difficult to comprehend. Within a few minutes, I had received a lesson in development, what partnership in development meant and about dignity in the process of development – a dignity that can be ensured only when we see everything as a true partnership and all of us as equals. And what is empowerment, if not a process of progressing towards equality in society?

Partnership is the fulcrum of capability approach to develop-ment. Partnership that is driven by a sense of equity and belief in equality, where the agency and the people look at each other as equal partners with a lot to mutually exchange. One where there are distinguishing contexts, strengths and roles in the process, but not distinctions that make one superior or inferior to the other. It is not easy for governments, NGOs and other institutions, or for that matter even individuals to shed the outlook of a 'giver', when they plan their interventions. At the same time, communities that are accustomed to 'receiving' without a choice, a say or the opportunity to question would also find it difficult to see themselves as partners and equal stakeholders.

Such a situation is obviously not desirable in the long run, and there is a need to transform the nature of transaction between the stakeholders. The onus of bringing about the change is on the state, civil society or other institutions that have professed development as their goal. It requires a new outlook, and preparation to handle new challenges and power dynamics within communities.

Flagship programs rolled out by the state like the National Rural Health Mission or the Mahatma Gandhi National Rural Employment Guarantee Scheme outline community involvement in planning or monitoring as an important aspect of the scheme. Its success however depends on how evolved the mechanisms to facilitate community involvement, and the ability to deal with different levels of community participation and inputs are. The state must look beyond token partnership of people in the implementation of the programs.

The same holds true for initiatives by NGOs. We must appreciate the fact that people's participation, inputs, choices and respect for those choices render the programs and their outcomes better. Conversely, lack of people's participation leads to lopsided development and fostering of conflicts and corrupt practices. The numerous industrial and infrastructure projects that have displaced people from their land and homes, siphoning off of large amounts of funds from welfare programs of the state, or inordinate delays in providing relief to victims of environmental injustice are examples of these.

Partnership also goes beyond just a program or an event. It involves dialogue that encompasses not just multiplicity of views, but also criticism, disagreements, emotions and other human sensibilities. When this is internalized by every stakeholder – the state and its machinery, the civil society, the private sector and common citizens – then we can claim to have embarked on a process of development with a true partnership approach.

Can you truly empower me?

It was early 1992. We were toying with the idea of getting the tribal women in Heggadadevanakote organized and forming small groups for them. The intent was to just get them together and talk about issues important for them. Later on in 1993 after Mamatha[12] joined us, we expanded on the agenda to include micro-credit and savings. I had no exposure to any issues concerning women and was using the opportunity just to stay connected and talk. The topics of discussion usually revolved around their health, their children, their husbands' drinking problems, or the issues they faced with the forest department. At times, these gatherings were also occasions for some local gossip. I would always try my best to attend these meetings and they are possibly my best learning experiences as far as understanding day-to-day challenges of rural women is concerned. The group was dominated by three very vocal Kadukuruba women – Selli, Sarasu and Somi. Shivamma, another Kadukuruba lady, would attend but not speak much.

We had been meeting regularly for nearly six months, when I started noticing that Shivamma was conspicuous by her absence. Her absenteeism became the subject of discussion and the women

---

12 Mamatha has been one of the key contributors to the growth of SVYM, especially through her tireless work with the tribal school. She had left her lecturer's job at an engineering college and joined SVYM in 1993 after reading an article about the organization in a Kannada periodical. She stayed with SVYM for more than a decade and then went on to work with the Karnataka State Child Rights Commission and subsequently, UNICEF ensuring that her passion benefits thousands of children across the state.

were quite vocal in criticizing her for this and saw no reason why she could not attend. They felt that I needed to intervene and talk to Shivamma and convince her that her presence in meetings was as important as her support in spirit.

A few days later, Shivamma came to our hospital with her youngest child who was sick. All her three boys attended our school and Ganesha, the eldest, was part of our first batch of twenty eight children. I met her and asked why she was distancing herself from the Sangha (group). I explained to her that empowerment meant making certain sacrifices and coming together was more than symbolic. I tried telling her that only through dialogue and discussion could each of us understand the problems on hand and think through a workable solution. More importantly, the collective could thrive only on the strength of the individual and the group needed every member's presence to make it work.

She gave me a patient hearing and casually mentioned that I would never understand her position. She told me that it was possibly much easier for me to attend these weekly meetings than it was for her. Seeing my puzzled look, she politely challenged me to spend a day with her and her family and then decide for myself. This was the first time that someone was testing my commitment and asking me to experience first-hand the issues that the community faced each day. I picked up the gauntlet and decided that I would spend the whole of the next day shadowing her.

What an experience it was! I walked up to her house early in the morning at around six o'clock. Her day had just begun and she was up and waking her family up. She spent the initial hours fetching water from the tube well nearby and must have made at least ten trips back and forth. Then she quickly gathered some firewood and lit up the hearth. The morning breakfast comprised food leftover from the previous day's dinner and was mostly *ragi* balls with chutney[13] made of chilies and onion. Once she made sure that all

---

13 A sauce made from a variable assortment of ingredients including coconut, vegetables, fruits and spices that is served with several South Indian dishes

her three children were ready and off to school, she and her husband walked to the forest nearby to collect firewood and bamboo. The life of the Kadukurubas revolves around bamboo; they use it for various purposes – from cooking to house construction to making small articles for daily use. She returned early with a head-load of dry firewood and was happy that she could find enough of it to keep the fires lit for the next two to three days. Her husband returned a couple of hours later with enough bamboo for them to work on for the next few days. Before I could even say 'rest', she was off to the river to wash clothes and bathe. After her return, she and her husband sat together and started splitting the bamboo and making them into strips that they could work on. As they worked, they also chatted and seemed to enjoy the company of each other. I realized that amidst all this activity, there was no lunch thrown in. Being hungry, I could not but help notice that they did not seem to be troubled at all. The children came back from school at around five o'clock in the evening. This was the indication for her to start preparation for dinner. From chopping the firewood, to cleaning the utensils, to fetching water to preparing dinner – she seemed to be fully immersed in her work. Before I could even have a decent conversation with her, I realized that it was nightfall. Amidst all this, she still maintained her calm and was always cheerful. But I was tired and desperately wanted to hit the bed. She would not let me go so easily. After the dinner that she served lovingly, she politely asked me if I understood why she could not attend the Sangha meetings.

It then hit me. What seemed like an ordinary task (making an hour for meeting every week) was indeed so demanding and expensive for these women. I had seen the Sangha from my point of view as a tool for empowerment and did not stop to ask myself what it could mean to these tribal women, without whose participation the Sanghas meant nothing. It was not just an issue of time and intent, but involved deeper dynamics.

After this incident, I started seeing these women through a new lens and my respect and admiration for them increased manifold. Shivamma had then told me something in her own simplistic way that rings in my ears even now. She had shown me that empowerment was not just about participating in weekly meetings and discussions, nor about seeking their rights and entitlements. For a woman, it was also about providing the physical, emotional and intellectual space and freedom, and a sense of stability and security. It could mean, depending on the context, ensuring that she had reliable access to water, fuel that did not demand going to the forest every other day and spending hours chopping it, and a livelihood with a steady income. It also includes the security that a good school for her children's education and a hospital that provides affordable healthcare to her family brings. Once this sense of stability and security is established, she would have the time and freedom to fully and effectively participate in the Sanghas or in any development process. I realized that unless these basic necessities are met, empowerment would mean little to the millions of Shivammas around India.

An important lesson this experience also holds for us is that empowerment is a multi-scalar process and how a collective responds to the process is different from an individual's response. Every individual's context determines their response to the process. The question to reflect upon is whether the process of empowerment itself is responsive enough.

A lesson in self-reliance

Medhi is a Bettakuruba[14] tribal woman whose life revolved around collecting bamboo from the forest. Bamboo was everything to her and her family. They would eat tender bamboo shoots, use bamboo for constructing their houses, and make different household articles out of bamboo and sell them to the local farmer. Bamboo was also used on special occasions such as for 'calling their spirits' or to make loud noises to drive marauding elephants away. Medhi had a small patch of agricultural land of around two acres, and along with her husband and three children, she lived a very contented life.

Medhi's house was located between the tribal hamlets of Brahmagiri and Hosahalli. Brahmagiri is the tribal hamlet where I had first moved in and started a dispensary before launching our education initiative, while Hosahalli is where we started the school for tribal children. For years, after every monsoon, I had seen Medhi and her family repair the thatched roof over their house. The house itself was a modest bamboo structure. It had been etched in my mind that they needed a more permanent structure to live in, and that she would definitely be a deserving beneficiary if any housing scheme was to be introduced.

It was in the early nineties that we started forming self-help groups for women. These were associations of women who would

14 Bettakuruba, meaning people or tribes of the hills are a forest-based tribal community living in Heggadadevanakote Taluk of Mysuru. In the list of scheduled tribes by the government, Bettakuruba community is called and classified as Kadukuruba, though Bettakurubas and Kadukurubas have slightly varying cultural identities.

come together to save money, discuss relevant social issues and try to address them, and also involve themselves in some income generating activities. Mamatha was overseeing this initiative and Medhi was a member of one of the self-help groups. When a housing program was initiated for these women, Medhi was one of the first persons who was asked if she needed assistance to get herself a more stable house to live in. There was, in our mind, no doubt about her eligibility to receive assistance and there was enough evidence of her need as well.

However, much to our surprise Medhi was amused. She had never imagined that the house she lived in was 'unstable' or 'unlivable'. Nor did she believe that the house we would provide her would be anywhere near what she would be comfortable with. Being quite intelligent, she asked us the value of the assistance we would provide. To this, we replied that it would be around twenty thousand rupees (about $330 US dollars at present conversion rates). Medhi had another simple but a thoughtful question that would unnerve any development sector professional. She wanted to know if we were interested in her having a comfortable home or were looking at providing her with what *we* believed to be just another house from our own stable of development schemes. Though this question was discomforting, we were wise, if not humble enough to agree that all we wanted for her was a house to *her* liking. It was then that she asked us in a matter-of-fact manner to give her the money and let her build her house the way she wanted it.

The disbelief on my face would have been very visible. As it is, I had felt exposed for my lack of understanding of the local context and the capabilities of the tribal communities. Houses, in my opinion, were to be those that professional architects, civil engineers and their ilk designed or constructed, and anything else would be short of acceptable. This was about to change. Medhi told me in her own polite way that she and her people had been living in more adverse conditions in the forest for centuries and knew how to take care of themselves. She felt that they had the knowledge and the skill to build themselves a good house, which she could augment with modern conveniences like roof tiles and cement plastered walls if she had a little extra money to buy them with. She wanted to know if we trusted her with the money to do exactly this.

I was relatively inexperienced in those days and I carried the false notion that I had the solutions to problems of the people. I was yet to learn the art of listening to people, understanding problems from their perspective and then coming up with solutions based on their strengths and needs. I did not know whether to trust Medhi to go ahead with her idea or impose my development framework. Hesitatingly, I agreed to advance the money to her and in return, learned some of the most crucial lessons in community development.

To my surprise, Medhi built a house, which stands to this day, much larger than what we were going to build with the same amount of money. Moreover, she built a house that saw the participation of her entire family in the process. They not only designed the house together, but participated in its construction every day. The entire episode was a revelation to me and taught me about building trust, about respecting others' perspectives and about heeding to the wisdom of indigenous communities. More significantly, the message of self-reliance that Gandhi wrote so much about was evident in the way Medhi carried her project off. From her quiet confidence to the intelligent questions, there was a strength that she depicted about herself as well as the community she belonged to.

Unfortunately, neither the government nor many NGOs under-stand this intricate and sustainable strength of the communities that many of us claim to serve. If listening to the communities deeply is made an integral part of the myriad schemes that we design for the communities, it would indeed result in a more evolved understanding of how to make development interventions work. Though we see a greater scope for communities to participate in development programs today, it is rare that their innate abilities and strengths are taken into account. From my own experience, or rather inexperience, I have come to believe that communities inherently understand, know, and are capable of their own development interventions. All that external change agents like us need to practice is to observe and learn from communities before forming our interpretations, and facilitate interventions that are contextually relevant and culturally appropriate. Towards this end, the lessons that Medhi and several women like her have for us carry immense significance.

Women, leadership and democracy

In the struggle for rehabilitation of displaced tribal communities in Heggadadevanakote Taluk of Mysuru district, I had come across many indigenous friends, both men and women who gave so much of themselves. Few women however matched Madamma, wife of Mudalimadiah, an elder chieftain of the Kadukuruba tribe, in tenacity and humility. Madamma was a pillar of strength during the entire process and could indeed be described as a 'queen mother' as she carried herself majestically, yet being extremely humble and very conscious of her indigenous roots. For years, she has been visiting the school for tribal children regularly and trying to ensure that the rich tribal knowledge, customs and culture are carried forward by the next generation.

Another woman who has been incessantly working to improve the conditions of her fellow tribal women is Bhagyamma. She is one of our women leaders spearheading the 'Self Help Group' movement in and around Basavanagiri, a colony of resettled tribal families, ensuring that self-help goes beyond mere sloganeering and micro-credit, and leads to real empowerment. Puttamma is another gem of a tribal woman who along with others waged a battle against the menace of alcoholism in her hamlet. Deeply aware of their ground realities and challenges, these women have shown commitment to and belief in the idea that a better tomorrow is possible for their communities.

Life in rural India revolves largely on the toils of industrious women, and it is difficult to imagine how villages can survive without them. Its children and families are fed, clothed and sheltered by women's labor. Its water and firewood are gathered by women's hands. Its families, farm and rural economy are productive because of women's work. Yet, they are accorded a lower social status and their work goes unrecognized, unvalued and unsupported despite their indispensable contributions in all areas of rural life. Along with donning the role of the traditional homemaker, a rural woman typically contributes significantly to the economy by participating in agriculture, dairy-farming and allied tasks, but is rarely compensated. Women who cook using firewood inhale smoke equivalent of twenty cigarettes a day and suffer from all the consequent lung, chest and eye diseases. And, if and when they are in control of their incomes, they invest almost all of it in the well-being of their children and their families, rather than spending on their personal requirements.

Likewise, their urban counterparts are increasingly contributing to society and the economy, and are participating in sectors and occupations that have traditionally been male bastions. From driving public buses to heading large corporations, from running NGOs to being senior bureaucrats, from excelling in sports to becoming leading academicians, scientists and engineers, we are now seeing women shine in positions and places of power and responsibility they have earned through tremendous struggle.

Women's contributions are desperately needed in the critical areas of the nation's well-being. The future of our nation depends on overcoming enormous challenges in health, education, nutrition, population and environment. Women bear primary responsibility in every one of these areas in their families and communities, day after day, and know best what needs to be done. Unfortunately, these realities have been reduced to only words that constitute politically correct statements. The true recognition or appreciation of the role and scope for women have not found expression in terms of participation of women in politics. While we've had a handful of women who've reached great heights as political leaders, women who've participated or are allowed to participate in politics do not constitute a large mass. The number of women contesting the elections from all the mainstream parties including those controlled by women themselves has been abysmally low and is a cause for concern. Post 2014 elections, we have 11% women members in the Lok Sabha, and this is the highest number of women Members of Parliament, India has ever seen. More than six decades after independence, it is hardly a number to be proud of.

We do get to hear several leaders and parties talk about facilitating greater participation of women in politics, but it seems that their commitments stop with discussing the women's reservation bill in Parliament and taking it no further. Reservation for women contestants within the parties itself a distant dream. We cannot realistically aspire to be a full democracy unless we find equal participation of women in the political sphere in the true sense.

However, the good news is that the inequity created by centuries of subjugation of women is being sought to be corrected in the rural hinterland of India. It was a historic milestone in India's journey of democracy when the 73rd amendment to the Constitution of India was made. In an unprecedented move towards decentralization, decision making powers and resources were transferred to the Gram Panchayats, the local self-government in the three-tier Panchayati Raj system. Even more historic was the mandate of reserving a third of the seats in the elected body of the Gram Panchayat for women, thus guaranteeing women a role in determining the future of their communities. Effectively, this meant transfer of power to one million women who would be elected as members of their Panchayat, many of whom are illiterate and have numerous societal hurdles to cross. It is perhaps the greatest experiment of sociopolitical transformation of our time. Nowhere else in the world is such a political process underway.

These women, who are continuously struggling against all odds to improve the lives of their families, their villages and the nation at large, are the key change agents for a new India. By ensuring that they gain access to the resources and information they need, and by allowing their voices to be heard, India can finally dream of becoming a nation with minimum gender disparities. There is no denying that there are obstacles ahead. Some political scientists observe that it is still men who seek to control power by proxy in these Panchayats and that women are reduced to being 'dummy' candidates. Acceptance of decisions made by women in positions of power especially in technical matters including budgets often require behavioral changes among others, indicating that women empowerment is not just about women. It entails changes in a system and society where gender disparity has been so much a part of everyday reality that it largely goes unseen, unexamined and unquestioned. Yet today, after thousands of years of suppression, the women of India are awakening to a new possibility – a future based on self-hood, equality and full participation. Despite the reluctance of the men and other hindering forces, it is a matter of time before more women enter the world of national and state politics and policy and leave their imprint.

Whether one desires it or not, whether one provides a legal framework or not, it is in the interest of the nation and its future that women take on leadership positions at all levels, especially at the grassroots. Women can quietly and meaningfully demonstrate a leadership that is at once humane and devoid of any political or electoral undertones.

Women can also challenge social norms in the manner that three women in a small village in South Karnataka collectively did, when an elderly woman of their village suffered without care and dignity.

Seethamma (name changed to ensure privacy) was a very poor and elderly bed-ridden widow in Mogarahalli village in Srirangapatna Taluk of Mandya district, about a hundred kilometers from Bengaluru. Her close relatives had stopped caring for her even as her condition deteriorated. She was drenched in her own urine and pus dripping out of her sores. The smell was so strong that one could not enter her room without closing one's nostrils. It was in this condition that the dedicated personnel of the palliative care unit of SVYM met her. They wanted to shift her to a center providing care for such patients, but her family members refused to allow this. A false sense of family pride and an eye on the little property that she had, made them immune to all the pleading of our staff. The local villagers and traditional leaders did not want to get involved. It was then that we were witness to the silent power of some concerned and committed local women.

Rukmini, Sundaramma and Komala, women members of the local Gram Panchayat were aware of the situation. They decided that enough was enough and took the family members of Seethamma to task. They berated them for not only neglecting her but also for preventing her from accessing care. They took matters into their own hands and had the Panchayat pass a resolution permitting Seethamma's transfer to the local care center. They did not stop with this; they informed the local police, mobilized resources from the village, cleaned up Seethamma and moved her to the Terminal Care Centre run by a humanitarian NGO in Mysuru. When I met these women to understand them and their motivation, I realized that there was no political undercurrent that was motivating them. Their concern was primarily about the well-being of a fellow human and the dignity and self-respect of another woman.

Democracy in India would be better served with the presence and rise of more such women, who can bring about the transformation that our nation needs from within. The political spectrum is yearning for such leaders, who would not only cleanse the system, but also bring in selflessness and a certain common sense, that only women possess. It is not just major political parties, but we as citizens as well who should pool in our efforts towards putting women at the forefront of making democracy work.

"CITIZENSHIP IS AN ATTITUDE, A
STATE OF MIND, AN EMOTIONAL
CONVICTION THAT THE WHOLE IS
GREATER THAN THE PART...AND THAT
THE PART SHOULD BE HUMBLY PROUD
TO SACRIFICE ITSELF THAT THE
WHOLE MAY LIVE."

ROBERT A. HEINLEIN

Governance, democracy and citizenship

Citizen engagement, democracy and good governance are all inter-connected and each one of them is responsible for the health of the other two. When citizen engagement thrives, it invariably leads to a vibrant democracy and eventually towards an environment of mutual trust, respect and accountability between the state and the citizenry. That, in turn can pave way for good governance and democratic functioning of the state's institutions. However, the interpretation of good governance and levels of citizen engagement vary widely between communities and so does the state's willingness and comfort levels with citizen engagement. In such a scenario, both the state and the citizenry have to step out of their comfort zones and take it upon themselves to create space for greater dialogue and innovative ways of engagement.

This section explores whether this is really possible given the changing and complex societal dynamics and raises questions that we as citizens must answer, more than anybody else, to ourselves.

What does 'good governance' mean to people?

When Mr. Siddaramaiah was sworn in as the twenty second Chief Minister of the state of Karnataka in May 2013, he immediately announced that his government would strive to be transparent and provide good governance along with a corruption-free administration to the people of Karnataka. This may seem like a customary declaration that any head of state would make upon assuming office, but for the people of Karnataka, who had for several years seen nothing but large scale political turmoil and mal-administration, even a nothing-out-of-the-ordinary announcement that brought attention to governance was a positive sign.

However, good governance itself may be interpreted in many different ways by different people. It is essential to carefully deconstruct the seemingly innocuous term to be able to better appreciate what it entails, and the responsibilities of citizens as well as the political class towards ensuring it. How the common man relates to good governance is determined by his day-to-day context and the meaning of the term is thus as varied as the contexts. My own experience and interactions with numerous people have unfolded a wide spectrum of interpretations of good governance by different people.

For Madi, an elderly tribal lady from Heggadadevanakote in Mysuru district, it simply meant getting her pension on time every month, instead of once in four to six months. Getting it on a monthly basis would make a big difference to her life. Transparency to her means that the postman delivering her pension would not take any 'commission' out of the amount that was due to her. All that Kariaiah, a small and marginal farmer, sought was good quality seeds on time, access to credit, reliable electricity and access to non-exploitative markets.

An industrialist friend had a different view. For him good governance simply meant better infrastructure support from the government. His view was that the government had to be an 'enabler' and ensure that the sector was supported with adequate infrastructure. He blamed the system for the crumbling infrastructure which included poor roads, poor connectivity, power outages and a lack of policy focus on developing industries. A fellow activist on the other hand said that having a pro-poor government with people-friendly policies amounted to good governance in practice. His view of transparency was guided by a vision of ensuring appropriate social accountability processes were built into every development scheme.

All that Ms. Sharmila, a housewife wanted was water and electricity throughout the day. She was concerned that intermittent power would affect the food in her refrigerator and watching her favorite tele-serial in the evenings. Muniswamy, a street vendor selling fruits in Bengaluru dreamed of the day when the beat policeman would not ask him for a bribe. Good governance meant that he would be able to save about twenty five rupees every day by not having to pay a bribe to stand and vend in the corner of a busy street. For Tippesha, who sells potted plants and mud pots by the wayside on a busy thoroughfare in Mysuru, good governance meant that he would no longer have to pay the city corporation authorities any money to trade his wares. It also meant that the corporation officials and local politicians would actually pay for the plants and pots that they took from him as and when they liked. For Ramu, a temporary driver with the State Road Transport Corporation, good governance meant that his job would be made permanent without having to pay the customary bribe of nearly five hundred thousand rupees. For many tribal students of Heggadadevanakote, who are the very first ones from their communities to have ventured into college, it meant access to hostels without harassment and getting their scholarship amounts on time, every time.

While the interpretations of good governance, transparency and a corruption-free administration for each of us are based on how it affects our lives, it is not enough to just dream about it or aspire for it without an understanding of what factors influence governance itself. We need to also understand what it truly means to have a government that is responsive, people-friendly and committed to providing good governance.

The concept of 'governance' is as old as human civilization itself. It includes establishing the process of decision-making as well as the manner in which the decisions are implemented and monitored. The concept centers on the responsibility of governments to meet the needs of the masses as opposed to select groups in society. It is a term now extended to describe how public institutions conduct public affairs and manage public resources. An analysis of 'governance' thus focuses on the formal and informal actors involved in decision-making and implementing the decisions made. There are state actors, which includes the government itself, its agencies and machinery, regulatory bodies and the judiciary that determine the style and type of governance. And there are non-state actors, which include lobbyists, influential capitalists, media, international bodies and financial institutions including international donors at one level and bodies like farmers' associations, co-operatives, NGOs, research institutes, religious leaders and political parties at another, all of whom play a role in influencing governance in different ways. Further, we must be warned and cognizant of the fact that groups with vested interests including organized crime syndicates, land mafia, etc. may also influence the process of governance.

According to the United Nations, good governance has eight major characteristics. It should be participatory, consensus oriented, accountable, transparent, responsive, effective and efficient, equitable and inclusive and should follow the rule of law. It assures that corruption is minimized, the views of minorities are taken into account and that the voices of the most vulnerable in society are heard in decision-making. It is also responsive to the present and future needs of society. The question however is, whether the government of the day and its machinery is conscious of these characteristics and cares to look deeper at how it can deliver on its promise of delivering good governance. It requires courage, commitment and the buy-in of all the key functionaries of the government.

Ushering in good governance would mean that the political and bureaucratic regime cannot operate in a 'business as usual' way. The government's authority in managing economic and social resources of the state would then be placed under public scrutiny and the use of discretionary powers would be minimized. Bringing in good governance would also mean that the capacities of governments to formulate policies and implement them will be monitored more closely, and both the political and administrative executive will be held accountable for failures.

In realistic terms it would mean that the political class cannot influence arbitrary administrative decisions such as transfer of officials. The executive will have the opportunity as well as responsibility to discharge its duties without fear or favor. Institutions such as the Lokayukta[15], the State Human Rights Commission, the Women's Commission and the Child Rights Commission would remain independent of state control and function as watchdogs in the true sense of the term. And importantly, policies would not be skewed in favor of individuals and groups with vested interests,

15 Lokayukta (meaning appointed by the people) is an anti-corruption ombudsman appointed by the state governments in India vested with powers of investigation on matters of corruption and mal-administration

private corporations, and instead be driven by a sense of equity and social justice.

At the same time, the demand for good governance from citizens cannot be termed as realistic without a will to participate in the process. The onus is on the citizens to make the governments responsive to their aspirations and for this, we have to look at ourselves and demand to be recognized as equal partners in the process. It would mean mobilizing people and resources in the form of time and attention to deconstruct and scrutinize decisions on development interventions by the government, demand justifications and base our engagement on reason and evidence. It is for us to make the 'authorities' take us seriously by making sure that we are aware of legislative frameworks, policies, programs and their provisions, allocation of budgets as well as spending. The more people engage in the nuts and bolts of programs, the simpler it would become to decipher the moves and intents of the state. Good governance is therefore a process of transformation where citizens evolve their role from silent onlookers to active agents of change.

The aspirations of Madi, Kariaiah, Muniswamy, Tippesha, Sharmila, Ramu and the tribal students resonate with millions of people across the country. Good governance is about meeting the expectations of all of them. However, the government cannot meet them without people's involvement, simply because a partnership approach is a key element of good governance. The Chief Minister's promise of good governance in the state cannot materialize if we, as citizens do not participate effectively and meaningfully. The onus of good governance is ultimately as much on the governed as it is on those who govern.

Empowered engagement versus enforced engagement

Community participation is no longer a buzzword in development. Decades ago, it was considered to be an innovative feature, one that NGOs spoke and wrote about in their project proposals for the consideration of grant making agencies. Over time, there has been a greater understanding of the power and potential of this paradigm, and now community involvement is an integral part of programs in the development sector. The government too has followed suit and has been providing legitimate space for different forms of community engagement in many programs. The 73rd and 74th amendments to the Constitution of India paved way for introduction of new structures for local self-governance in the form of Panchayats at the village, block (Taluk) and district level as well as local bodies in the cities. Consequently, community participation in monitoring of government programs has necessarily meant that citizens engage with these bodies. Questions however exist on the scope and effectiveness of community participation, the right processes for enhancing community participation and more importantly, whether the government is driven by a genuine intent of empowerment even as it continues to prescribe structures for citizen engagement.

For a start, what does the state envisage as the level and extent of community participation? Can communities actually participate in the manner desired by the state? Can the extent of this participation be measured and if yes, what are the metrics? Can the level and nature of community participation be included as an integral part of program outputs and outcomes? How does community involvement influence the programs itself in terms of their implementation and delivery of outputs? The answers to these questions are not easy, but there are examples and experiences that provide some clues.

In 1990, the Government of India started a decentralized and participatory program called Joint Forest Management to involve local communities in the management and conservation of forests. Subsequently, the state government in Karnataka introduced the Joint Forest Protection and Management Program (JFPM) in the state, the announcement of which was made with a lot of fanfare. The program aimed at setting up local committees for protection of forests that would take collective decisions on various local issues such as fencing, collection of non-timber forest produce, and participation in conservation efforts of the Forest Department. The guidelines for the composition and functioning of these Village Forest Committees (VFC) were laid down by the government. Thanks to the keen interest shown by the then Chief Minister of the state and overzealous officials, it was announced that three thousand committees would be formed in the state within three months.

What happened in reality was that local forest guards, who were the first points of contact with the community for the forest department, ended up writing names of people they knew and submitted those lists to the department. As a result, close to three thousand VFCs did emerge on paper, but how many of them were 'true community' groups, is anybody's guess. Today, virtually none of these groups have survived, and JFPM remains a wasteful reminder of how things should not be done.

The National Rural Health Mission, launched by the Government of India in 2005 tried to emulate many success stories of community involvement across India, especially from the experience of NGOs.

There have been quite a few NGOs that have been able to give credible and functional space to communities in their programs, which are reflective of community aspirations. In an attempt to recreate this 'good practice', the Ministry of Health and Family Welfare mandated the formation of local committees at different levels to participate in decisions and monitor action related to health and sanitation in their villages. Prominent among these committees, at least in terms of the attention they received, were the Village Health and Sanitation Committees (VHSC), now termed Village Health, Sanitation and Nutrition Committees (VHSNC). The Government of Karnataka and a few other state governments went a step further and introduced multi-year programs in collaboration with NGOs for spreading awareness and mobilizing people on the ground to form these committees and actively participate in their functioning.

Although these efforts have resulted in some promising examples of how communities utilized the knowledge and status provided by these platforms to drive changes in the villages, the larger picture is dismal. Despite the empowerment initiatives introduced and large sums of money spent, most committees are either non-existent, exist only on paper or are dysfunctional. There are numerous committees where memberships are offered as political favors and where members have practically no awareness on their roles and responsibilities. This may be attributed to the fact that there are untied funds that the committees receive every year, and the lack of awareness among communities at large makes it possible for the funds to be siphoned off. Therefore, what the government has managed to do is some excellent 'isomorphic mimicry'[16], but has failed to factor in and provide scope for the intensive and

---

16 Isomorphic mimicry, wherein forms and structures of functional states and institutions are adopted by others, while camouflaging a persistent lack of function has been regarded a technique of failure by Lant Princhett, Michael Wookcock and Matt Andrews in their working paper: Capability Traps? The Mechanisms of Persistent Implementation Failure, published by Center for Global Development.

contextually relevant 'behind-the-scenes' processes that NGOs and CBOs[17] employ for making community participation work.

The government needs to understand that groups or communities that sustain over a period of time are often the ones that evolve organically. The corollary is that expecting community action to sustain through the imposition of orders with uniform guidelines from the top are bound to meet with failure. While the government is indeed taking the first and important step of mandating committees and laying down norms for equitable representation of people in them, it must account for the fact that certain combinations would be resisted and the power dynamics within the group will have an impact on its functioning. Community engagement is a subtle and long drawn-out process, which cannot be enforced externally. Nor can one expect communities to respond or perform in a pre-determined manner. One can, at best, work towards creating a conducive environment for communities to dialogue. The process of enforced engagement must give way to empowered engagement and this not only requires contribution from people, but demands persistence and patience from the government.

Vigilance Committees (VC) of the Public Distribution System (PDS) in the state provide another example of a conceptually wonderful initiative, the failure of which may be attributed to inadequate preparation. These committees, whose members are none other than the users or beneficiaries of the PDS, are supposed to be watchdogs of the Fair Price Shops (FPS), the retail outlets under the PDS. The committees have been set up to ensure that the distribution of food grains to people followed the prescribed norms, both in terms of quality and quantity. Should these Vigilance Committees perform well, leakages in PDS can be plugged to a significant extent, thereby ensuring food security to thousands of

17 CBO - Community Based Organizations, usually non-profit collectives directly working with communities at the grassroots on development issues and representing them in various forums. CBOs are also often staffed by members of the local community that they work with.

poor families. The ground reality however is that most of these committees are defunct, while many of them are populated by relatives and friends of the shop owners. Such collusion, in addition to being a bad example of how community engagement should be brought about, is also an impediment to the process of bringing in transparency and accountability in the system. During an investigation I carried out into the irregularities of PDS in Karnataka, I came across instances where the members of Vigilance Committees got a share of the 'spoils' in the form of a few kilos of rice and a few liters of kerosene from corrupt FPS owners.

It is indeed ironic that these Vigilance Committees now need to be under a vigil. We are left to wonder if this situation could have been avoided, had more attention been paid to the structure and function of community participation. Adequate training and capacity building on the roles and responsibilities with a stress on active and ethical engagement from the members of these committees is rarely a strong feature of the programs that are supposed to foster community participation. In fact, the lack of it could be seen as another facet of 'enforced' community engagement.

Contrast this with the manner in which School Development and Monitoring Committees (SDMC), committees comprising locals formed to monitor the progress of government schools have evolved over a period of time. Here, we are provided with an example of how communities can be associated with a program that positively impacts their lives on a daily basis. My experience of working with thousands of such groups across the state of Karnataka shows that such groups can be made to work effectively if one pays attention to the selection of members, their training, and stays engaged with them continuously. The key is to identify and develop a stake for them in the program that goes beyond mere token participation in meetings. I know of many active committees that have gone beyond their stated mandate, the members of which take pride in participating in the school's progress with a zeal to make sure that their schools are some of the best in the local areas. This is not to say that SDMCs are functioning well universally, but the fact that the government has persisted with the concept consistently and for a long time is a favoring factor in whatever success we've seen so far.

Another kind of community engagement that now has the legislative mandate is social audit in the Mahatma Gandhi National Rural Employment Guarantee Scheme (MNREGS), India's flagship social security program that guarantees a minimum of one-hundred days of employment to eligible men and women in rural areas. Social audit is a transparent and collective review of records and progress of programs often conducted jointly by civil society organizations, communities and locally elected representatives. It is an extremely progressive concept and tool in the hands of communities and something that no other program or scheme from the government has been able to incorporate on a large scale. There are rumors that the powers that be are getting increasingly uncomfortable with the tool and may bring in changes to the process and curb the role of communities even as they get used to the idea of demanding accountability from the system. Such changes, if introduced would only be an impediment to community empowerment. An empowered community always has the potential of going beyond a specific program such as the MNREGS and start auditing other government initiatives as well. Such empowerment is bound to unnerve the government, especially when states are unwilling to support and accommodate community participation beyond its cosmetic value. Though a fair bit of preparation and a certain degree of maturity and readiness is needed from the communities for handling the tool, social audit is an excellent manifestation of community empowerment and participatory democracy.

Technology in the hands of communities is also an empowering tool when used for planning and monitoring public services that they are entitled to. When rural communities in Mysuru district were trained to answer a questionnaire on facilities and services made available to them by their respective Primary Health Centers, we found that they were not only consistent in their participation, but went one step further. Participating in the monitoring activity motivated these communities to engage in dialogue with the local doctor and other stakeholders to find solutions to issues ranging from shortage of personnel to emergency medical transport and resumption of water supply to the health centers so that minor surgical procedures could be conducted. This project showed how technology can be a gateway to enhancing the quality of engagement while also leaving communities empowered. The key however was a sustained process of facilitation and capacity building by a team that was sensitive and responsive to the local socio-cultural and political dynamics.

Community action in planning, monitoring and governance is indeed needed, but it has its share of challenges. In rural settings, Gram Panchayats are the de-facto space for communities to engage in and most committees such as the Civic Amenities Committee (CAC), School Development and Monitoring Committee (SDMC) and Village Health, Sanitation and Nutrition Committee (VHSNC) are accorded the status of sub-committees of Gram Panchayats. At times, tension brews between elected representatives and members of these committees. The former believe that they are the chosen ones to articulate the aspirations of the communities that they represent and resist these neo-groups that are emerging under various government programs, even though they are members of these groups too. Social and political divides within villages can also be seen manifesting themselves in the functioning of these committees and no government led mechanism or process can effectively address these issues. It is only a community led process with the possible involvement of civil society organizations committed to grassroots democracy that can reconcile these tensions.

I feel community engagement needs to evolve spontaneously to be legitimate as well as relevant, instead of being introduced to fulfill a requirement under some scheme or program. One needs to allow for social dynamics to play out in the formation and functioning of these groups rather than insisting on rules of engagement as construed by bureaucrats sitting hundreds, if not thousands of miles away. One also needs to pay adequate attention to both the structure and the functioning of these groups and invest in training them to meet their logical ends. One must be conscious that a one-size-fits-all approach does not work in the process of community engagement as every community and its context is unique in its own way and has a bearing on process outcomes. We need to understand their underlying complexities and allow time for these groups to mature in order to perform effectively. Setting strict time-frames and pushing the groups to achieve program outputs can be counterproductive to the larger vision of community empowerment, for it would then become easy to dismiss the concept without visible changes in defined time-frames. In fact, it is the processes that need greater attention than the milestones. Empowerment is subtle and cannot be enforced as it would only serve to retain or increase power distances between communities and 'authorities'. Likewise, we can ill-afford to sacrifice 'empowered engagement' in our attempts to usher in 'enforced engagement'.

Renegotiating citizenship

In the month of October 2014, police personnel in the city of Delhi suffered a series of unrelated assaults. In different incidents one police constable was gunned down fatally, two others were fired at, and the Assistant Commissioner of Police himself was assaulted by three persons that included a juvenile and a woman in an incident of road rage. Around the same time, there were protests by the general public against legitimate actions of the police in Mysuru city when they tried to enforce traffic discipline. In nearby Mandya, a woman Deputy Superintendent of Police was nearly run over by alleged henchmen of the sand mafia only because she was trying to do her job and enforce the law.

Despite being independent incidents, one wonders if there is something common about all of them. Is the rule of law disappearing in a country that is presumably democratic and law abiding? Why is 'power' being so despised? Can these incidents be dismissed off as isolated events or should we see the pattern of 'state control' weakening? Or is there a lack of space for people to engage with the state constructively and meaningfully, which prompts people to act in a way that pushes the situation towards lawlessness?

There is no doubt that people, not only in India but around the world in general, have lately found the need to express their disgust with authorities, as indicated by the incidents of shoes being thrown at politicians and others, who are seen as symbols of power. While the right to dissent is sacrosanct in a democracy, we have also seen that vandalism and damage of public and private property often accompany protests and *bandhs*[18]. We need to reflect upon who can truly be held responsible for the losses and disruption caused by these incidents.

The failure of the state in keeping unruly elements under check, and act in an accountable manner is often to blame, and rightly so. In many instances, we have seen the high and mighty go about transgressing the law with impunity, whether it is in the form of large scale corruption, rash driving and traffic violations that are at times fatal, various forms of human abuse or organized crime. In other incidents, self-styled moral policemen and vigilante groups have routinely carried out violent acts and ended up assaulting men and women ruthlessly on the pretext of protecting culture. Then, there are incidents like the stampede in the state of Bihar during the celebration of an annual religious festival in October 2014 that left dozens of people dead and hundreds injured. The tragedy is attributed to the poor management and under-preparation by the officialdom, but it is difficult to fathom if anyone will be held accountable for the incident at all. Expectedly, angry protests by relatives of the victims had followed.

There are questions galore beginning with what is the state's role as regards to ensuring governance in situations where its citizens go out of control. Should the state use its power to enforce discipline on a 'mob' that refuses to see prudence in following the law? Or should the state show restraint and minimize the use of force with a view to foster an atmosphere of dialogue, even when people don't seem ready for it? Is it possible to strike a balance between the two approaches? There are questions that probe the role of citizens as well: why do citizens show scant respect for the law, unceremoniously ignore and disrespect it and ultimately make governance a casualty? Is it really born out of a disillusion with the state and its

18 Bandh (Hindi) is a general strike used as a form of a protest by political organizations including political parties, trade unions and others that results in suspension of business and functioning of institutions.

mechanisms that have failed to deliver good governance? Can we, as citizens see to it that vested groups do not take advantage of the general disenchantment with the system? While both, the state and its citizenry have critical questions to reflect upon, it almost seems that the two entities are on diverging paths.

Contrast this with the Prime Minister holding a broom and calling upon his fellow citizens to take on the task of cleaning India. We need to interpret this not as a call for 'cleaning' India, but as a call for a collective expression of 'citizenship'. To know whether it can really happen and whether we can truly express ourselves fully as responsible citizens of a vibrant democracy, we need to understand and appreciate our socio-cultural DNA and our political evolution over the last few centuries.

From a disparate set of kingdoms to acquiring a national identity of 'India', it has been a long drawn-out political process for the nation. While the control of power and responsibility of administration may have shifted, the mind-set and engagement of citizenry has not evolved proportionately. Credit for the formation of the modern Indian state must go to the East India Company that framed the laws to administer it. But one needs to appreciate that these laws were framed to enable control of the state over its subjects rather than ensure accountability of the state to the citizenry. We were only subjects of the British Crown and were never regarded as its citizens with our rights and entitlements. This changed in 1947, when we got our independence and the state became answerable to the citizens of India. We inherited robust and well-meaning institutions of governance that were considered to be some of the best in the world along with laws framed to address different contextual needs. Though we seemed to show some promise in the initial years after independence, we have gradually allowed degeneration to creep in over the next sixty years resulting in an unhealthy and noisy democracy that we are today.

It is said that those who do not learn from history indeed will be condemned to repeat it. We need to learn what the history of our country reveals. India is historically known to be a weak state but one with a strong society. Noted German philosopher Hegel had observed: "If China must be regarded as nothing else but a State, Hindoo political existence presents us with people but no State." Traditionally, we have never conceded power at a deeper level to our so-called 'rulers'. Today, we are in the process of transitioning from this traditional mind-set to that of accepting democratic norms which demands a degree of subservience to the 'state'. Post-independence, a fragmented group of kingdoms and provinces combined and merged became a chaotic democracy. What we have today is a loosely structured, segmented, federal union with the central government sharing powers with the states but not so much with the citizens. Gunnar Myrdal, the Swedish economist had dubbed India as a 'soft state' based on the government's inability to get things done. This is reflected in how the arms of the state have demonstrated repeated failures in enforcing the laws and legal frameworks. Whether it is handling corruption, keeping criminals out of our political system or having a fair and transparent criminal jurisprudence system, enforcing the rule of law on the high and mighty, to having effective regulations in the public sphere – we have seen how the state has been ineffective in evoking trust and faith in its functioning. A 'soft' state, Myrdal further wrote, is unwilling to 'impose obligations on the governed' and there is correspondingly 'unwillingness on the part of the governed to obey rules.' What we are seeing today is not only a low level of social discipline but also a system that has incentivised lawlessness and is very forgiving of social and legal transgressions.

Given this scenario, we now need to not only see and understand the lack of citizen engagement and social accountability, but also look at ways of renegotiating citizenship itself and its spirit. Citizens need to own up to power and responsibility and see themselves as part of the state and also appreciate the state's limitations. What we have today are either docile and unaware citizens, indifferent citizens, or those active citizens who are unforgivingly critical of the state. Those wanting to foster an environment of dialogue with the state are few and far between. One wonders if it is too utopian to expect our citizens to be partners in progress with the state and accept their roles and responsibilities within the constitutional framework of the state and its institutions.

The state also needs to appreciate that the spirit of citizen engagement, once evoked, can no longer remain a mere political slogan or a tool to garner public support. Enlightened citizens will soon begin demanding good governance and participation, as a matter of entitlement and the system needs to be prepared to respond suitably and sensitively. Otherwise, what will result is a society filled with disgruntled elements that will further marginalize the state and push its weakness into a state of chaos, irrelevance and confusion. The state's role in renegotiating citizenship is therefore centered on accepting its flaws and winning the trust of its people, and being open to criticism and voices of dissent.

Today, India as a nation, stands at a critical juncture in determining whether active citizen engagement would thrive in the world's largest democracy, or if it would be overpowered by forces that let asymmetry of power prevail. It will be judged by how the state has played its role in facilitating greater citizen engagement, initiated and instituted social accountability practices and made people look at themselves as equal partners in the nation's development.

Where everyone is a victim

In 2010, I was appointed by the Lokayukta, Karnataka to investigate allegations of corruption and mal-administration in the Public Distribution System (PDS) in the state. While the investigation unearthed large scale leakages and corruption that was making a severe dent in the state's exchequer, the experience has been one of immense learning for me. I traveled the length and breadth of the state and met hundreds of people and was convinced that 'corruption' leaves everyone feeling like a victim.

The owner of the retail unit of the PDS or the Fair Price Shop (FPS) lamented that he needed to keep everyone happy to be able to survive. Everyone, for him included the Food Inspector, the local politician, the village headman, the members of the Vigilance Committee who monitor his shop, and the people who loaded and unloaded the food grains from the trucks. And in order to keep them happy, he bent or broke laws, violated the rules of the department and even ignored guidelines set by the Supreme Court of India. He was typically unwilling to disclose information on the number of cardholders, their entitlements, or his stock position publicly. Bills were hardly issued and even if issued, were unreadable and erratic. The quantity and quality of food grains issued were mostly below standards.

During the entire investigation, I did not come across a single Fair Price Shop in the state that issued the allotted amount of rice to the cardholders at the stipulated price. It was usually two to four kilos less than their entitlements and sold at varying prices despite the uniform prices being fixed by the government across the state. The shops that are required to be open throughout the month with one weekly holiday were usually open for four to six days a month and the timings were rarely followed. With all these deviances from the norms, the FPS owners still considered themselves to be victims and when questioned would respond that they were paid very little commission, forced to distribute more grains to people than the actual number of legitimate cardholders and that palms had to be greased on a regular basis to keep out of trouble.

Moving up the chain, the transport contractors who perform the important task of transporting grains from the godowns (warehouses) openly disclosed that contracts were awarded to them only if they were in good books of the officers who make these decisions. And that came at a price. It was also an excuse to siphon off grains during the transportation process to make sure that adequate money is made to take care of these 'incidental expenses'.

Next in the chain were the wholesalers who managed the godowns. The godowns themselves were in pathetic conditions with poor quality of storage and there was an indiscriminate use of pesticides at these facilities. What was surprising was that the inventory at these depots, worth millions of rupees, were managed manually. This, in a state deemed to be the Information Technology capital of the world. One officer confided in me that people were apprehensive that computerization would make things traceable and the system would demand good governance. Keeping things gray and opaque was in their collective interest. The wholesalers for their part felt that they were victims as they were pressurized by the local politicians to donate grains whenever there was a local event or a fair and ensure that people attending them were well fed. This was their ruse to divert food grains meant for the thousands of poor families in the state.

The summer months are the ones when the entire officialdom is anxious, and under pressure. The months from April to June are usually those when officials are transferred to different locations. Unwilling to take the trouble of relocating, finding schools for their children and moving out of their comfort zones, the 'victimized' officials pay enormous sums of money to the powers that be, to avoid uncomfortable transfers. They then use this as a justification to subvert the system for their own gains.

The political class is a whole breed apart. Their tryst with corruption begins with bribing the voters to elect them. They feel victimized every time they need to contest an election. From winning elections to keeping their constituents happy throughout their term, the pressure on them to spend money is very high. This for them is enough justification to dig into public resources with utter disregard and contempt for any rules that may prevail.

Whoever I met and interacted with – from the common man on the street to the higher authorities and political leaders – have felt that they are victims of a system, which they found easier to fall in line with, rather than stand up and fight. This is an example of a systemic failure to provide good governance, where everybody feels that s/he is a victim. However, the real victims in the chain are those poor and marginalized families who are denied food grains because their entitlements have been eaten away at every level in the chain. It is a shame that one calls himself a victim while indulging in an act of corruption that leaves a system on which millions of families depend for their food security, ineffective. What may be also noted is that at every level in the chain, one had easily forgotten that s/he is also a citizen with duties and responsibilities and it is their neglect of duty that results in hardships for fellow citizens elsewhere.

Amidst this scenario, we have heads of state promising transparent and corruption free administration. How would a Chief Minister or a Prime Minister back his promise of good governance in such a scenario? Would it be possible for the head of the state to investigate every irregularity in the system, even if we strengthen anti-corruption measures? It is ultimately the accountability of citizens to fellow citizens that can keep a nation on the path of progress. And when one is in a position of power, s/he should rather consider it an opportunity to prevent the system from corroding further and breathe fresh life into it, rather than deeming oneself a victim.

"So long as the millions live in hunger and ignorance, I hold every man a traitor who, having been educated at their expense, pays not the least heed to them!" uttered Swami Vivekananda, the great monk of India. It is worth reflecting upon and realizing who the real victims of our actions are. Bringing about good governance is indeed challenging, but we need to look for reasons to keep the system fair, clean and transparent, rather than find excuses for our failures. After all, the fight *against* corruption may be dubbed as a fight *for* good governance.

A social transformation led by India's Prime Minister

One hundred days after Narendra Modi became the fifteenth Prime Minister of India and likewise, a year after that, both the print and electronic media were abuzz with their own views on how the government has fared and how the government needs to run. The by-line *Achhe Din Aanewale Hain* (the good days are coming) used by the Bharatiya Janata Party in its successful election campaign of 2014 invoked plenty of references in television debates that critiqued the government's performance. The line itself means different things to different people depending on who is using it. One needs to appreciate that measuring the performance of the government and by extension the public agencies that constitute it, is a complex and long drawn process and cannot be 'oversimplified' by mere survey questions or by relying on the limited knowledge of professional television commentators.

Hundred days, or even one year is arguably too short to demonstrate any concrete change or impact. At best, one can only comment on the direction in which the government intends to proceed. That being said, it is indeed frightening to understand how 'vague expectations' in the minds of the common people are now turning into 'urgent demands'. Let me narrate a couple of incidents that highlight how people are extending their own internalization of a personal problem into a larger societal one.

It was a little more than three months since the new government was formed at the center. I was traveling by an auto-rickshaw in Mysuru and got into a conversation with the driver. He was expressing his anger at the state of the roads in the city and despite Dasara[19] celebrations being only a few weeks away, how little was being done to improve them. He was angry that despite the nation having seen hundred days of the Modi government, the roads had not improved at all. I was both amused and intrigued at how involved he was in a civic issue, but how limited his analysis of the problem was. For him, driving on the streets of Mysuru was an everyday necessity, and the health of his vehicle as well as his own depended directly on the health of the city's roads. What was fascinating was how he was seeing this problem and who he was holding responsible for the situation, and furthermore who he was expecting to provide a solution. My explanation that the local city corporation and by extension, the state government being responsible for the Dasara celebrations were to be held accountable did not seem to make much of an impact on him. Another good friend was narrating how on a recent trip to Mumbai, he got talking to a taxi driver ferrying him around. The taxi driver was lamenting that the daily traffic jams he encountered in Mumbai showed no signs of easing, despite the Modi government completing hundred days in office.

Both these incidents may seem trivial to a few, but then they illustrate the everyday reality for these people. It is this reality that drives their interpretation of 'Achhe Din' and good governance. Each one of us will have our own ways of understanding and interpreting the change that was assured to the citizens of India, but is it fair to merely transfer these problems to a 'messiah' and wait for him to wave his non-existent magic wand? Can we measure

19 Dasara or Dussehra is an important annual Hindu festival celebrated across India, Nepal and Sri Lanka. Dasara celebrations in Mysuru has a grand history of more than 400 years and the festivities, which include an elaborate procession of Mysuru's royalty, elephants and tableaus are a global tourist attraction. Dasara has been accorded the status of a state-festival in Karnataka.

the performance of the central government and the Prime Minister merely based on the problems that we confront as citizens at a local level and our perceptions of the 'good days' that was promised?

We must take an unbiased look at some of the decisions that the Prime Minister and the new government took in the first few months. These included internal actions like empowering bureaucrats to take decisions and make them accountable as well. The Prime Minister sought to introduce changes in the style of the government's functioning keeping the urgency and importance of demonstrating both efficiency and effectiveness in governance. After a long time, we saw the Houses of the Indian Parliament function well and exceed many efficiency parameters without being stalled frequently. In terms of rolling out programs and schemes, launch of Digital India, the scheme for financial inclusion and *Saansad Adarsh Gram Yojana*[20] were noteworthy. Despite some shortcomings, the launch of these schemes indicate an intent to bring long-term changes. It was also important that the new government continued with some of the welfare schemes introduced by the previous regime. Attempts to rejuvenate SAARC and the formation of the BRICS bank, a firm stand at the WTO without succumbing to global pressures and the dissolution of an outdated Planning Commission and replacing it with a body that promises cooperative federalism were other notable positives in the first few months of the new dispensation.

These were issues on which only the central government could have made decisions; issues that the common man could not relate to, or experience resulting changes, at an everyday level. The improvement in the investment climate, the proposed investments from different parts of the world and a bullish stock market could be seen as positive indicators for the economy. The PM's intent of letting the work speak for itself rather than rely on media releases,

20 *Saansad Adarsh Gram Yojana* is a program launched by the Prime Minister of India towards holistic development of villages led by the Members of Parliament in their own constituencies.

especially in the first couple of months after coming to power could also be regarded as a good development for governance.

However, one needs to go beyond all these, and into the process of citizen engagement and appreciate the kind of transformations occurring in the country. By ousting the previous political regime, the people of India had clearly and consciously communicated this social undercurrent in an electorally decisive manner. It is only natural for people to then seek an expression of their personal aspirations through a public response from the government. This expectation is further compounded if people believe that the government will bring a 'magical panacea' for the issues that matter to them. The current demographics and the economic aspirations of a hungry, restless and impatient young population add to this collective expectation. Further, all these expectations seem to be pinned to one man at the helm of the government rather than the system and all its components that need to function well for changes to happen.

That a social transformation is taking place in the country and that it is connected to the change of power at the center, which includes the election of Narendra Modi as the Prime Minister of India needs to be acknowledged. The fact that an 'outsider' like Modi from a very humble background and without any 'dynastic' connections came to occupy the highest post in the country is a sign that people's abilities are outmatching traditional and established societal parameters of political success such as caste, class or political dynasty. This is despite newer influencing factors such as the role of big businesses in not only funding elections but in shaping the policy climate of the country. Further, social values and community dynamics are also changing, thanks partly to technology and media, giving rise to newer problems and complexities. When the existing repertoire of solutions is no longer sufficient to overcome these problems, it is natural that a restless generation externalizes the issues and looks to a charismatic leader like Modi, expecting him to solve the problems expeditiously.

Keeping aside questions such as whether it is fair to expect one person to deliver on all expectations or whether the present government can be criticized for failures that have a deeper connect to the past regimes, let us look at how the Prime Minister has responded to the expectations. He has displayed his intent to connect with people, if his public speeches including the address to the nation on Independence Day, his interaction with school teachers and students on Teacher's Day, or his regular radio shows on different issues are anything to go by. The content of his speeches often relate to the personal uneasiness and explicit troubles of individuals: unemployment, price rise, cost of fuel, personal learning, stress of examinations, etc., and urge people to convert their indifference into involvement with public issues at local and national scale. Encouraging people to participate in the Clean India campaign, Clean Ganga mission, appeal for societal peace and harmony and a call for a moratorium on religion and caste based violence for the sake of progress are examples of this.

We also see that the government is seeking to actively engage the average citizen via social media and portals like MyGov.in where people are being invited to provide suggestions and policy inputs. The Ministry of Health and Family Welfare put out its draft National Health Policy in the public domain for inputs and the Railway Ministry sought responses from people on key issues before finalizing its budget in early 2015. These must be looked at as windows for dialogue provided by the new government, which, considering how closed the policy making process has been in the past, are positive developments.

It is against this backdrop that we should assess the response from the citizens and what they need to do further. My conversation with the auto-rickshaw driver and his refusal to accept information about the role of citizens in civic issues throws light in this direction. Citizens are not necessarily suffering from a lack of information; in this digital age, information often dominates their attention. What is needed is the ability to discern, reason and learn to shift perspectives from the 'personal' to the 'societal'. The PM has in fact been subtly asking the citizens of India to enhance the width, depth and scope of their capacity to engage with matters concerning their own development. The question is whether, as a society that is rapidly transforming itself with newer values, priorities and issues, we are able to add this dimension in our engagement with the state. It is up to people to co-create dialogue forums and build their own capabilities to use information and reason, for engaging with the state. Not doing so will be a missed opportunity, but sadly, we may still end up blaming the Prime Minister and his government in the event of failure.

This government has earned its fair share of brickbats as well. From being overzealous on the issue of land acquisition ordinance to its handling of dissent in civil society, from the purported dilution of environmental laws to cuts in budgetary allocations to critical sectors like health, education, child welfare, rural development and Panchayati Raj, there are issues where the government has distanced itself from the collective opinion of civil society and development priorities articulated by development sector organizations. These have expectedly evoked criticism from civil society, but how the government responds to criticism would be a crucial component of the transformation of the state's engagement with its citizenry. At the same time, it is important to build the capability of ordinary citizens to engage with the government to counter these developments in a non-confrontational manner.

As an electorate, we have shown that we can be decisive as well as unforgiving. We now need to raise our levels and display enormous sociological imagination and enhance our role in civic and governance matters. The Prime Minister seems to be cognizant of this fact and must show the leadership in facilitating a constant increase in the level of citizen engagement. At the same time, citizens also need to show ownership, innovativeness and responsibility, and take advantage of the windows of dialogue while constantly pushing the government to do more. That would be a step in the direction of taking India to the status of a full and healthy democracy.

"THE NEW SOURCE OF POWER IS NOT MONEY IN THE HANDS OF A FEW, BUT INFORMATION IN THE HANDS OF MANY."

JOHN NAISBITT

Information indeed is power – people and their right to information

The passing of the Right to Information (RTI) Act in 2005 was an important milestone in the history of democratic India, which conferred upon common people the right to request information from any 'public authority'. This Act, comparable to the Freedom of Information Act (USA) has tremendous potential to tackle corruption and asymmetry of information in public, and it is therefore imperative that every citizen of the country knows about this act.

SVYM undertook a campaign-on-foot to create awareness about RTI among the people of some 120 villages in 2008. Covering five districts in South Karnataka, the campaigners interacted with thousands of people in about a month on not just people's right to information, but also on different issues related to democratic development including corruption, accountability and citizen's responsibility. This section provides a glimpse into that momentous undertaking of the organization and is dedicated to the hundreds of staff and volunteers who participated in the walk and most of all, to the rural community of this part of India, whose hospitality and warmth provided us the motivation to carry on and conclude the campaign successfully amidst a host of challenges.

Today, the success of the RTI Act can be gauged by the fact that it is under constant pressure from the powers that be – to be amended, diluted and made to lose its relevance. Only relentless citizen engagement can ensure that we do not concede the grounds that have been gained through tumultuous times and hard sacrifices of people.

A walk for information, a walk for power

'Information is power', especially in the context of rural India. In our experience of more than thirty years in the development sector, we have repeatedly seen that people who are able to access information and process it effectively for their use are the ones who get out of poverty more easily, while the others are merely condemned to cope with it. Disparities and inequalities have grown in the past decade, but some of the flagship social security and poverty alleviation schemes of the government have also provided opportunities, which when effectively utilized could transform the lives of individuals and communities. For instance, the concept of social audit in the Mahatma Gandhi National Rural Employment Guarantee Scheme is a powerful tool that village folk can now use to demand information about how the program has fared in their villages and who has really benefited. Similarly, the passing of the Right to Information Act has pushed the boundaries of democratic citizen engagement and is a potent tool that can reduce corruption and enforce good governance practices in public service delivery institutions.

It is ironic however, that though we live in the information age, people are deprived of information and awareness about the very tools that are supposed to break the asymmetry of information. With the specific aim of reaching out to people and equipping them with information related to the Right to Information Act and related issues, a group of people from SVYM decided to walk a distance of nearly four hundred and twenty kilometers from Saragur in Heggadadevanakote Taluk of Mysuru district to Bengaluru, the bustling capital of the state of Karnataka. Reaching out to more than 200,000 people in about 120 villages and towns across five[21] districts in the southern Indian state of Karnataka, the campaign titled *Jaagruthi Yathre*[22] commenced on the 4th of September 2008 and culminated on the 2nd of October, 2008 – the date of Mahatma Gandhi's birth anniversary, also known as Gandhi Jayanthi. The year 2008 also marked the twenty fifth year of Swami Vivekananda Youth Movement and we saw this campaign as a fitting celebration of our work at the grassroots over the quarter of a century.

Following an enthusiastic flag-off, the team set out on foot from Saragur covering about ten to twelve kilometers every day throughout the campaign, though there were days when more than twenty kilometers were covered. A team of young enthusiasts from different parts of Karnataka traveled on bicycles ahead of the team on foot and helped in mobilizing the people in the villages and preparing them for the ensuing interactions. We stayed overnight at the villages and slept in schools, temples, on porches and sometimes in the open, accepting whatever the villagers had to offer. During the night stays, the team performed street plays and had group discussions with the villagers on local development issues, besides apprising them about the RTI Act, social audit and MNREGA, and in some places about entitlements under the Public Distribution System. These were accompanied by distribution of pamphlets and selling of nominally priced books on the RTI Act and how it can be used.

The entire campaign was apolitical and non-confrontationist in its approach. What's more, it was the resources mobilized from

21 5 districts: Mysuru, Chamarajanagar, Mandya, Ramnagar and Bengaluru Urban.

22 *Jaagruthi Yathre*, meaning journey of consciousness, also referred to as *Yathre* in this book, was the title given to the campaign undertaken by SVYM to raise awareness about RTI Act and other issues among people.

the villages that funded the event and fueled us with energy and motivation as we walked from one village to the next. It was the locals who provided us with food and accommodations, and their hospitality egged us on. There were days when it was planned well and there were also days when we landed at villages with no idea of where we would get our food from or where we would stay, but almost miraculously somebody somewhere was able to make a breakthrough and ensure that we were secure and ready to move on. People were encouraged to walk from their own village to the next. It was also an opportunity for the walkers to discover themselves and become aware of their own inner selves. Anybody subscribing to the concept was welcome to participate in the campaign and walk for as long as they liked.

The campaign was indeed an experience of a lifetime for many of us and replete with events and incidents that infused us with inspiration as well as humility. It brought us in touch with a reality that is out of the ordinary for a vast majority of the urban-educated world. Vinay Krupadev, one of the volunteers from USA shares: "after walking about a hundred kilometers in eleven days and speaking to hundreds of people in villages and cities, I've absorbed so much of what this country is about." He further sums up the experience by saying: "By the second day of the *Yathre*, I began to see that this walk wasn't just about the Right to Information Act; it was about restoring hope in democracy. We were walking to remind people that things could change and that they had the power to be this change." Indeed *Jaagruthi Yathre*, which translates to a "journey of consciousness," was more than a walk for building community awareness; it aimed at creating an environment of positivity, where people would truly believe in the inherent power and goodness of community action and take on the responsibility of cleansing the system instead of merely complaining against it. And, with tools such as the RTI Act, one could truly transform the way the people could engage with the state.

A revelation of contradictions and hope

The fact that millions of people in the country are deprived of basic amenities is routinely deliberated upon in meetings and conferences by governmental as well as non-governmental agencies. However, an understanding of what it means to actually live without toilet facilities or access to water and a deeper appreciation of grassroots realities can only be had through experience. We can then realize that lack of drinking water and sanitation, children out of school or inadequate nourishment are not mere statistics to be quoted in meetings, but serious life issues for the people in the villages.

The fourth morning into our month-long campaign to bring about community awareness on RTI was one to remember. We were at a village which hardly had any households with toilets and when I was faced with the need to use one, the only recourse was to find my own private spot and also search for water. The experience was a revelation of the reality of lives in rural India and the associated hardships that prevail even after six decades of being a 'socialist' country. At the same time, it was also a revelation of the genuineness of concern among the people. When one of the local villagers saw my predicament, he ventured to help me find a secluded place and also provide water. I realized that the hospitality of these people was not limited to receiving us and providing food to eat and a space to camp for the night.

We saw how our villages are a model of contradictions of the modern world. People seemed to have the money to buy set-top-boxes[23] and brand new motorcycles, but were hardly ready to spare a thought about the lack of toilets in their houses. They wanted to dress well and flaunt the latest mobile phones, but not worried that their children were not learning much at the local school. The struggle to find a balance between growing needs of a modern existence and fulfillment of basic requirements that would indicate better human development was evident. With regard to the latter, a sense of helplessness and loss of self-esteem was perceptible and it seemed like people were used to accepting what came their way and had resigned to the situation. It was easy to feel angry and helpless at how the only choice that the rural citizenry seemed to have is being in a state of constant tension and conflict, or a resigned acceptance.

Yet, from our interactions, we were happy to note that the youth wanted to know and understand how different things work. They were hungry for the information we were giving. It was an indicator that the people were not happy with the status quo and that there is a desire, albeit unarticulated, for change. The genuineness of their hospitality, the patient hearing they gave us and the engaging questions were indeed a positive sign. It seemed like a contradiction when juxtaposed against the helplessness that is often expressed in discussions on development issues.

These contradictions however may be explained by the way development schemes have been implemented in rural India. The state's planning and executing machinery has little time, patience or competence to understand the dynamics and power structures in the rural areas and also little appreciation of attitudinal and behavioral dimensions. This results in shoddy implementation of schemes and does not provide enough space for meaningful partic-ipation of the people. What is further disturbing is that all these

23 A set-top-box or a set-top-unit is a digital appliance that converts / decodes digital signals from external signal source into content that can be displayed onto a television set.

schemes are often prescriptive, rather than dynamic or responsive, and seem to be 'urban solutions' to 'rural problems'. Precious little consideration is given to the skills, knowledge and practices that could help in addressing rural issues through grassroots perspectives.

These observations give us an idea of how relevant the campaign that we undertook was. It had the potential to connect an unexpressed desire for change with tools that could actually be employed to drive changes. The hunger for information coupled with their genuine hospitality could only mean that our village folk still believe that change is possible and that they can be a part of that change. It also tells us that we need to be making an investment in building the confidence and self-esteem of rural India along with building its infrastructure. Our campaign was a step in that very direction.

This was reaffirmed in the debriefing meetings of the campaign where every member of the team spoke about their experience. Instead of feeling overwhelmed by the daunting challenges they had witnessed along the way, they reveled in it and spoke about how different and life-changing the *Yathre* had been for them. My conviction that values can only be taught by living them was playing out in reality. As one interacted with these young people, one could feel that the future is safe in the hands of enlightened youth driven by values. It was a revelation after years of institution building that we have to accelerate the task of 'people building'.

Blending with the villages and their issues – some reflections

Normally, campaigns like the one we undertook have one central message to be disseminated among the people. It is also natural that the team focuses on that message and constantly seeks ways of delivering it more effectively. However, in our walk for community awareness on the Right to Information Act and other tools of socio-economic empowerment, we chose to blend ourselves with the villages we walked through or stayed in, and also understand the issues and local contexts better. This was often spontaneous, but helped us communicate with the people in a contextually relevant manner.

Starting from Saragur in Heggadadevanakote, we had traversed through more than a dozen villages in a week and were moving towards Chamarajanagar, a district that borders Mysuru on the south eastern side. Before reaching Chamarajanagar town, we stopped at a village named Shivapura. We performed a street play in front of the Gram Panchayat office of the village and had about a hundred people watch the play. What we got to see in return was something more remarkable. Not far from where we staged a play on the Right to Information Act, a tool that could bring transparency and accountability in public services, a mobile van was stationed through which people were openly selling grains from the lot that were meant to be distributed under the Public Distribution System (PDS). We were witnessing first hand, an act of corruption in the PDS, one of the world's largest food subsidy program on which millions of poor in India depend, and were aghast at how it was being carried out with impunity. It was a live example of how corruption is eating into the vitals of this nation, but the bigger tragedy is that people seem to have taken it for granted and have stopped reacting to such adverse events. Corruption has become a way of life and not being corrupt is an aberration. But could we, who were on a campaign to fight corruption remain mute spectators?

Our way of response was to form a human chain protesting against corruption in public life once we reached the heart of Chamarajanagar town. Hundreds of locals joined us and we walked together along the main street of the town. We urged people to resist corruption by being aware of the provisions of programs and schemes. I had little knowledge at that time that I would later take up a Lokayukta investigation into irregularities of PDS in Karnataka that exposed deep flaws in the system and huge losses to the state due to leakages.

Continuing our campaign in Chamarajangar district, we reached a village called Mangala, where we were confronted with defiance from the men in the village. They were denying us a space to carry out our activities in their village. After half an hour of coaxing and negotiations, they relented and allowed us in. The team performed a street play, sung a few songs and I interacted with the villagers. It turned out that it was merely a reaction to a local political issue that had resulted in some people obstructing us in our campaign.

My reflections of that day still hold true to a large extent. The villages of India are today plagued by the evil of local politics. Decentralization is not as visible in development as it is in politicking and corruption. Large political egos even in small villages often come in the way of contextual development. Further, politics in rural India is dominated and controlled by men. Despite all the empowerment processes that have been initiated in various ways for women, men still control the social, political and economic direction of a village. The lesson we could draw from the experience was that one has to factor in local political dynamics while working in villages and to consciously keep inclusion and empowerment of women as an undercurrent of all development interventions.

This *Yathre* also showed us the reality of caste divides prevailing in rural India. At many places, we saw people wash the hand-pumps, which our team used to drink water from, and use a bit of cow dung to 'purify' it before and after we had used them. Access to homes and even their toilets depended on the villagers making sure that we belonged only to their caste. Many a time, the women campaigners were denied access to the toilets even in times of dire need only because we refused to disclose our castes. It is a tragedy that so many social reformers have come and gone, but people continue to bask in the security of their own castes and accompanying beliefs. Very few have the courage to break these barriers and usher in a spirit of freedom from forces that are hindering our progress.

We had realized that it is just not physical strength that one needs to take on such challenging endeavors. One also needs an enormous amount of emotional and intellectual strength to do such things. I found myself more emotionally and intellectually drained because of what I saw and how much more needs to be done. More than six decades after independence, we have not been able to provide basic amenities to our people, though we are on the verge of going to the Moon and Mars.

We also encountered the bane of alcoholism in the villages we traveled through. A little more than half way through our campaign, we were walking towards Malavalli Taluk in Mandya District, where we had learnt that consumption of *Neera* (a local liquor) was rampant. Alcoholism is a disease that destroys families and potentially the lives and futures of children, especially so in rural areas. We decided to raise our voice against this nuisance. While most of our battles against alcoholism in the past had centered on the men who consume liquor, in Malavalli we encountered a newer dimension of alcoholism. We found that consuming *neera* was not just a prerogative of men here, but of women as well. Many women, we learned, demanded *neera* as part of their daily wages, especially in the paddy belt. Unlicensed alcohol stations dot the rural horizon with the production and sale of alcohol being controlled by powerful elements. Neither the state, through police or excise department, nor the local communities see it as a problem and as a result, hardly take any action despite the knowledge that the liquor being traded and consumed was illicit. We took it upon ourselves and convinced the police to take action and despite facing some resistance, were able to destroy the liquor in possession of the traders. We knew that this action would not bring any lasting changes, but hoped that some people might be inspired to act further on the issue. The laxity on the part of the law keepers was appalling, but the inaction from the citizenry could not be ignored either.

Among the various topics we touched upon – RTI, MNREGA, PDS – it was PDS that people could immediately relate to the most. This is a scheme that possibly touches every family, especially in rural India, but is corroded by corruption and lack of awareness. Most of the beneficiaries did not know what their entitlements were, the price they needed to pay for the food grains and how the PDS outlets called Fair Price Shops operated. Through our campaign, we tried to fill such information gaps among people whenever the opportunity arose.

The multitude of issues at hand and their complexities at times seemed so daunting and overwhelming that it was easy to lose hope. But every time the chips were down, it was someone among the people who would boost our belief. One evening, we were at a prayer gathering in a village called Hosahalli, when a large number of children joined us. The setting was an open one in the center of the village with three temples and a *Mutt*[24] surrounding

---

24 Mutt or Matha (Sanskrit) is a monastic or religious establishment in Hinduism and a few other religions of South Asian origin and is usually headed by a spiritual or religious leader of the sect or order. Mutts are also known to be philanthropic

us. We had a good street play performance that day. One of the villagers, Nanjappa, who was also the erstwhile president of the Gram Panchayat, spoke on corruption and politics. He brought out the perspective that the community needed to be a watchdog for politicians and hold them accountable. He stressed that the incentive for politicians to become corrupt was the illegitimate and corrupting demands of the community itself. His call to the community was to become honest before demanding honesty of their elected representatives.

This message connected the people gathered for the event as well as the campaigners to a reality that was possible. We can only demand accountability when we are upright and aware. Ultimately, true empowerment is about reducing the power distance between the rulers and the ruled. The Right to Information Act does just that.

institutions, and their activities extend from offering food and shelter to the needy to establishing educational institutions and hospitals.

Ningamani, the citizen

The word citizen is often attributed to an anonymous non-descript individual whose identity is merged among a mass of people. Citizen's movements, and for that matter many other campaigns driven by organizations and individuals that comprise 'civil society', rarely have narratives that go beyond equating citizens to this anonymous non-descript individuals. What happens when we give a name, a background and a description to this citizen whose rights, welfare or development are supposed to be the premise of the whole movement itself? How do we discover whether the movement has meant anything to the individual citizen in the long run?

Ningamani was one of the many individuals I had an interaction with during our month-long *Jaagruthi Yathre*. Though not a long one, it was a memorable exchange, something that fills me with humility and inspiration every time I remember and reflect on it, even today.

It was the 18th of September 2008. It was also a fortnight into our campaign-on-foot to spread awareness about people's right to information by engaging with the communities. We were marching towards Sattegala village in Mandya district and had reached what the local villagers called the Sattegala circle – a busy intersection. There were a lot of people milling around the many petty shops that abounded this area. The sun was blazing with all its might and I was feeling tired and hungry. I spotted a shady tree and went and stood under it to regain some energy. I found an elderly lady there, selling flowers. Beside her sat a young girl, who I thought might be her grand-daughter. Seeing me, she asked me what I was doing there. Hesitatingly I explained to her my mission and was hoping that the conversation would be short. Ningamani – her name as I discovered later – would not let me get away so easily. She wanted to know why I was carrying so many books with me and what was in them. More out of courtesy than out of wanting to make her aware of the RTI Act, I briefly explained to her the act and told her how it could be used to get things done in a rural area. I also told her that the book would cost ten rupees. What left me surprised was her spontaneous response. She told me that since I had walked such a long distance for a good cause, she had to encourage me and buy a book from her meager income. For a moment, I felt touched by her compassion, but silently wondered what this old illiterate woman would do with the book.

I found my answer a couple of months later. I had asked my colleague Shekar to travel along the same route again to find out whether our walk had made any impact on the lives of thousands of people that we had met and interacted with. As he reached Sattegala circle, he found Ningamani sitting at her usual spot and selling flowers. He met her and explained why he had come. Ningamani was overjoyed on seeing him and gave him a warm hug and a joyous welcome, much to Shekar's surprise. She explained to him how, many months ago, an elderly person (I hadn't realized how old my gray hair had made me look!) had sold her a book for ten rupees. Having paid virtually a significant chunk of her day's earnings, she had taken the book home and got her grandson to read it for her. On learning that she could find out why her widow pension was being delayed, she had made him write out an application on her behalf. She had, in fact, made an application to the Tahsildar under the Right to Information Act, asking why it was taking more than four years for her to get her rightful entitlement, her pension. A week later, the local village accountant met her and gave her the pension orders. She was as surprised as she was delighted. Instead of getting an answer to her query in the application, she received what she needed and what she had waited a long time for.

On hearing this from Shekar, I realized how powerful this act was and how well one could use it to usher in development and create an empowered rural community. Apart from the relief and happiness of having received her pension, one can only imagine how powerful this elderly, illiterate woman would have felt in being able to move a bureaucracy that was insensitive and non-responsive to her all this while. It reveals how the act could pave way for a participatory democracy in which citizens proactively engage.

Ningamani is that citizen for whom this campaign was conceived and undertaken. Ningamani represents the emergence of a resurgent India – an India where every citizen feels equal to everyone else and gets the government machinery to treat them equally and with dignity. She bears testimony to the change that will eventually overpower a corroded system, and give true power to people, regardless of how slow and silent the process is.

Ningamani has since passed away, but she leaves behind a legacy which our current political and bureaucratic system will have to respond and become accountable to. She also showed that the anonymous non-descript citizen matters and can gain from being aware of their rights and entitlements. To meet and empower a thousand Ningamanis was the true goal of our campaign.

The cities and the villages

Very often, we complain that our villages lag behind cities in terms of development because of the lack of amenities and facilities that are supposed to make the quality of life better. There is an aspiration among the village youth to migrate to the cities to make a living and partake of the fruits of development. Our month long walk of four hundred and twenty kilometers to build awareness on Right to Information Act among the larger community gave us a glimpse of many differences between our cities and our villages. These were differences, not just of infrastructure and facilities, but of culture, attitude and behavior among others.

Towards the end of our campaign, we approached Bengaluru, the bustling metropolis of South India. The rural countryside landscapes were making way for busy industrial and commercial complexes and densely populated localities. We could see heaps of plastic and trash every now and then at an ever rising rate. The noise and the activity increased as we neared the city. So did the cynicism and apathy of the people. The commercial mindset of people was evident. One person argued with us that we could not be undertaking this *Yathre* merely out of national interest. He felt that we must be having our own political or financial interests in this exercise. Our explanations could not convince him or make him accept our perspective. That was not so much a concern to me as was our evident lack of trust in each other. How could we hope to build democratic structures and processes without mutual trust?

Going by our experiences in this campaign, building social capital based on interdependence, reciprocity and trust seemed to be much easier in rural India than in urban areas.

Bengaluru is also known for its traffic snarls and we encountered our first traffic jam near the town of Kanakapura, caused apparently by a political event. It was after losing much time and patience that we managed to reach the bus stand and our team sang a few patriotic songs there. Time is a premium commodity in the cities, yet it seems that we spend less and less of it productively and meaningfully.

Our interactions became all the more brief as we neared the city. In fact, some people that we tried to interact with curtly asked us to be brief. Some bought our book on RTI more to end the conversation and see us off rather than out of genuine interest in the subject. Life in general seemed to be superficial and shallow with no real regard for fellow citizens who are trying to strike up a conversation. Apart from a general disdain towards civic action, I even got the feeling that these people were manifesting cynicisms, apathy and indifference more as coping mechanisms, a veneer to cover up their superficial existence and inaction.

We had not expected that having more of our material in Kannada, or rather a lack of enough material in English, would be a limitation in Bengaluru. With the city having become more cosmopolitan over the years, it seemed that knowing Kannada, especially to read and write the language, was an exception rather than the norm. A few instances also left us wondering whether conversations in Kannada were an inferior way of communicating. Laina Emmanuel, a volunteer who joined us in the campaign from Delhi shares "very few people in Bengaluru admitted to knowing Kannada. It was in a way good for me, because I felt I could use my strengths in getting the message across. But other team members felt left out. I unwittingly contrasted the villages and the city again. When I went to a village, people helped me out, I did not feel inferior because I did not know Kannada, just different. People made sure I learned and were patient enough to teach me."

I am convinced that language is not merely a tool of communication in rural India. It is a manifestation of the underlying rich culture and allows for a strong emotional narrative of the people. Whereas urban areas have begun to see language as a tool for transaction and a skillset to facilitate their business needs, the usage of which is driven by market pressures. I wonder if the connection between language and its cultural legacy would dwindle over time, especially in the cities.

While it is true that cities and its inhabitants have their challenges, it is disheartening to note that they somehow manage to rob one of the warmth and affection that we are inherently capable of showing. Our villages manage to show it despite poverty, poor amenities and lack of 'development'. We can only hope that the apathy and indifference we came across in urban pockets are not universally spread across all our cities. Our supporters who live in the cities and believe in us, and our work are testimony to that hope. Civic action groups in the cities are increasing by the day, but they need to be supported consistently by a critical mass of people to be successful in whatever they do. While it may be easier to build awareness among urban citizenry, thanks to their education levels and a host of communication tools that we have at our disposal, converting that awareness into meaningful citizen engagement is a challenge. The rural scenario, on the other hand provides a contrast, where it is possible to mobilize a greater proportion of people through consistent efforts and engagement, and work towards addressing local issues.

In either case, citizen action can be successful only with a belief in the 'collective' and mutual trust. Laina was asked during the campaign "Where did you find the courage to come for this walk without knowing a single person?" Her short answer was "I believe in the basic goodness of people. I believe if you are nice to people, they would be nice to you."

The culmination, the new beginning

The day had finally arrived. In one month, we had come quite a distance, both figuratively and physically. The walk of nearly four hundred and twenty kilometers had not left us as exhausted as I had initially presumed. It had been an arduous journey, but the support of the people along the way had helped keep us energetic and in high spirits. It had also been a journey of self-discovery. The simple lifestyle, absence of television and newspapers, lack of basic facilities, interactions with thousands of people had all taught us so much. Most importantly, they had reinforced our faith in the innate goodness of mankind. It had also given me personally, the time and space to look within. The campaign had provided me with the opportunity to see things as they were and not as I wanted them to be.

Many of our friends and well-wishers joined us on this day. Some of them walked the last stretch with us and others joined us at the Gandhi Statue on Mahatma Gandhi Road in Bengaluru, where our campaign culminated. Many of them were exemplary citizens, who in their life and times have given new dimensions to citizen engagement. Nikhil Dey from Mazdoor Kisan Shakti Sanghatan, the Rajasthan based collective that was a pioneer in the national movement for Right to Information, walked with us on the last day. It was also an honor to have Justice M N Venkatachaliah, an extraordinary champion of human rights in India at the emotionally charged function organized to conclude our month long *Jaagruthi Yathre*.

At the function, Justice M N Venkatachaliah was at his usual inspiring and witty best, and spoke on how this *Yathre* had restored his faith in societal transformation. My friend and co-traveler from SVYM, Dr. M A Balasubramanya started with excerpts from the Kannada translation of one of the songs dedicated to Swami Vivekananda, the great monk we draw our primary inspiration from. We also sang the Kannada version of 'Where the mind is without fear...' from Tagore's Gitanjali. I spoke on the act, how it can transform India and its rural areas, and on how we can use it as a tool to bring in development and good governance; Poshini spoke of her experiences and her perspective on how the act can affect the common man's life; a senior bureaucrat from the Government of Karnataka read out a passage from an article on Satyagraha by Mahatma Gandhi. Nikhil Dey spoke on how activists had worked tirelessly for more than ten years to get this act see the light of day and how we need to be watchful to ensure that the act is implemented both in letter and spirit.

This was the first Gandhi Jayanthi that I celebrated with the people I admired, adored, respected and loved. This was the first time that the occasion had meant so much to me. The goodness in the air was palpable. The hope and expectation that we had generated by this walk now needed to be maintained and raised. How wonderful it was to see people of all ages and all walks of life come together and feel so positive and hopeful!

Though this function was about celebrating the culmination of the campaign, this movement was never an event meant to have an ending. This whole struggle had been scripted to be a continuous movement to usher in our basic right to demand good governance. As citizens, we could no longer be satisfied with mere information, we all had to work to ensure that we can have a society that is free from fear; a society where the meekest shall find their voice; where the rule of law is no longer an exception; where every citizen of India shall be proud to participate in its development and play his or her role in making India a healthy, vibrant, inclusive and participatory democracy.

Beyond the campaign

No campaign can change the world overnight and it is unwise to have such expectations despite the energy and euphoria generated. At the same time, one must not feel let down by what may seem as a dip in enthusiasm after a campaign as eventful and inspiring as the *Jaagruthi Yathre*. SVYM's campaign to spread awareness about RTI Act and other developments that were intended to better the lives of millions had concluded, but the commitment to the campaign's goals remained. The purpose of any campaign is to act as a force that triggers change, no matter how painstakingly slow and challenging it is. It is to inspire people to take action and convert the high energy and strength of the collective that is seen in the campaign further, to smaller but lasting changes. One can imagine the campaign to be a big torch from which, at the end of its journey, a hundred candles go out in different directions.

It was not unexpected that people asked questions about what we planned to do after our month long campaign-on-foot. Some even questioned the wisdom of our walk and whether the effort was worth it. All we could say was that every step mattered, and every single person who joined the campaign made a difference.

Following the campaign, we received more than fifty telephone calls every day at an RTI cell set up by SVYM. Personally, I received more than fifteen calls each day from different parts of Karnataka indicating that there were many people out there wanting to know more about this act, looking for guidance on how to use the act effectively, and how to appeal when the officials in-charge of giving out the information do not respond. People called us to know if we could go and extend our activities in their areas, or if we could train them and their teams to take on this task. Some even asked us if they could join our crusade in some way.

A few senior government officials also called me up and spoke to me. They wanted to know why I had got involved in such activism at this stage and how this could be the harbinger of pressure on the system. They politely discouraged me from taking this any further. A local Member of the Legislative Assembly of Karnataka called me and asked me why we were insistent that the people of his Taluk collect information on all ongoing schemes that were in different stages of implementation. He wanted to meet me and get me to understand the difficulties that he was facing because of all this. I could sense that people's queries were putting pressure on the system and there was this question whether the pressure was undue. My response was to consider these developments and questions as the beginning of change and a beginning of processes that will slowly and surely change the way governance is understood in this country.

After the campaign concluded, we planned a set of follow-up actions. A small team was constituted that would travel again, this time using vehicles, through most of the villages covered in the campaign over a week and talk to some people that we met during the walk. This was to try and understand whether and how our *Yathre* had made any difference to people's lives. We also trained a few youth in each Gram Panchayat, who would act as RTI resource persons in the Taluk of Malavalli in Mandya district in December 2008 with the help of a local NGO. The intention was to sustain the process of empowerment that begun with the campaign. In the month of January 2009, similar resource persons were trained in the entire district of Gadag in North Karnataka to make RTI a people's movement in coordination with another local NGO.

Back home in Heggadadevanakote in Mysuru district, we undertook a two year intensive program on RTI awareness, usage of the act for development and for pre-empting corruption along with social audit processes. The intended impact of this program was to use the RTI Act to make the Public Distribution System of food grains transparent, effective and people-friendly. We also wanted to make this a model Taluk in terms of RTI awareness across the state. We wanted to usher in a new era of participatory democracy in the villages of HD Kote through this project. In a span of two years, we could see changes at the grassroots level in terms of communities having better awareness of their entitlements and traders operating in conformance with the rules.

The spirit of the campaign neither ended at the concluding event, nor with the closure of projects and initiatives undertaken thereafter. We realized that this *Yathre* can truly be a grassroots revolution, and hope that people elsewhere in India will emulate it in their areas. The purpose of this *Yathre* would truly be served when common citizens take it upon themselves to be better informed, and inform others of provisions and programs, their workings and irregularities, their strengths and limitations and their impact on fellow citizens. After all, we live in the information age, and reducing the asymmetry of information is a necessary precursor to reducing the asymmetry of power.

"TO OPPOSE CORRUPTION IN
GOVERNMENT IS THE HIGHEST
OBLIGATION OF PATRIOTISM."

G. EDWARD GRIFFIN

Citizen engagement and the fight against corruption

India's post-independence history is dotted with many civil society movements – for rights, for justice, for inclusion and for civil liberties, and quite notably the resistance against imposition of Emergency Rule in the mid-seventies. Though these movements found support from students, activists and others, they were built on the participation of people who were directly affected or leaders with distinct political leanings. The year 2011 was a momentous one in that a section of our society, hitherto reticent about participation in public action took to the streets in a popular movement against corruption. At its peak, the campaign had a singular focus of having a legislation against corruption passed by the Parliament of India. A new voice had raised itself against the monster of corruption and despite its flaws, the movement against corruption has undeniably changed the political landscape of India in its wake and aftermath.

I was not to remain unaffected by the developments myself. Having been pained at how corruption is eating away our nation's development potential, it was an opportunity to lead a solidarity action in support of the movement from Mysuru. I also had the advantage of proximity with the leaders of the campaign at the national level, but it was the strength of local people's participation on which our movement took off and thrived. This section brings forth glimpses of the movement along with my thoughts on corruption, the battle against it and what it would take to curb the menace.

The reality of corruption

Sometime in early 2014, an elderly woman called me from Bengaluru asking for help in saving her small plot of land and a house bequeathed to her by her late husband. She told me that a few people had been pestering her for many months and asking her to sell off her property to them, which she did not want to do. She was living on a road close to the new international airport on the outskirts of Bengaluru and the real estate value in that area had escalated significantly. It was evident that the pestering had gradually turned into intimidation and one can easily imagine the state of helplessness and vulnerability that this woman could be driven into. Being a couple of hundred kilometers away, the first thing I could do was to politely suggest to her that she approach the local police. I was surprised by the anger in her voice when she replied that she had already done that. The police apparently had told her that she should be happy that these people were at least offering to buy the land from her and willing to offer a decent price, instead of perhaps driving her away using nefarious means. All I could do was to listen to her and feel her anger, pain and sense of helplessness.

Another young lady, a domestic helper who had also lost her husband called on me within a few days of this incident, to thank me for securing a pension that was legitimately hers. It was nearly a year and a half earlier that she had come to me for help to secure her widow pension. Being very poor and having two daughters to take care of, she was well within the norms prescribed by the department and was eligible to receive a monthly pension. It was after more than fifteen months of intense and relentless follow-up, that we managed to get the order for her pension.

She had come to me with a packet of sweets to thank me for the help and casually mentioned that she had gone to the local post office to get her first month's pension of four hundred rupees. I was surprised and wondered why the amount she received was lower than the five hundred rupees stipulated by the government. When I asked her about it, she innocently replied that the postman who delivers the pension to her door-step had told her that the pension would be five hundred rupees if the money was directly credited to her account and four hundred rupees if it came through the post office. She not only believed this, but also was convinced that there was logic in the explanation. I was dumbstruck at the sheer candidness of not just her narration, but the manner in which things had transpired.

I was also wondering if she could have got her pension sooner had I let her negotiate with the system on her own. All that she needed to do was grease the palms of the local officer and the expense might have been well worth it. The price of trying to work the system honestly was a delay of more than twelve months and six thousand rupees lost from the pension that she could have otherwise received. The 'fee' to be paid to one of the 'agents' who had promised to get the monthly pension started within three months of her husband's death was just half that amount. I was left seeking answers to many questions. I was also wondering how many million poor and innocent people in this country live their everyday as victims of this all-pervasive corruption.

As I narrate these incidents, my mind is drawn to another incident that took place in my own family more than thirty years ago. I was still a medical student and we had just finished celebrating my sister's wedding. A couple of weeks later, I found my father very distraught and worried. I learnt that he had received a notice from the Income Tax department asking him to explain how he had the money to buy jewelry worth twenty thousand rupees[25] for his daughter's wedding. My father was then a Senior Audit Officer in the Accountant General's office in Bengaluru. Having been in service for nearly thirty years and being a senior gazetted officer, it was not unreasonable to reckon that he could have surely saved enough money to buy jewels worth twenty thousand rupees. He had himself, being a very duty-conscious public servant, disclosed this purchase to his department as per established procedures. He was upset that a law-abiding citizen like him who had paid all his taxes and done everything by the rulebook had to be subjected to the humiliation (in his view) of receiving a notice from the Income Tax department. I could understand how he must have felt. This was the same person who would not even drink coffee offered to him at the office where he was conducting an audit. Even that gesture of courtesy was for him, unacceptable. That was his standard of ethics in public life.

While the first two incidents are reflective of how deep rooted corruption has become, the stress that my father endured despite being upright and honest to the core is an indication of how the system is riddled with obstacles for someone who refuses to tread the corrupt path. And today we live in a world where we have simply built the cost of corruption into our transaction. Ranging from local needs such as getting construction plan approvals or a driving license to large scale industrial and commercial requirements like allocations of band frequencies to telecom companies or the permission to drill for oil or natural gas, everything comes at a price. In the public sector, job postings, promotions, transfers as well as avoidance of transfers are determined by the amount one is willing to pay rather than merit. Corruption has become such an integral part of our lives that we do not see the negative consequences of such actions.

It is not uncommon to find that building norms were violated

25 20,000 rupees would be equivalent to about 320 US dollars at prevailing conversion rates

or that the fire department overlooked the inadequacies while granting clearances after a major building collapse or fire in a public building. Nor is the inefficiency and stubbornness of staff in utility companies an uncommon experience for those consumers who are not willing to pay a price. Traffic violations are deftly handled by both, the violators as well as the traffic police, if money passes hands quickly. In every sector that we can think of, corruption usually begins with the user looking for a shortcut to maximize his gain in quick time. Very rarely does it occur to us that we, as a nation are the final losers in this sprint to make a short-term gain. From the corrupt politician that we elect after being 'bribed' to do so, to the traffic violations that we want condoned by the local policeman for a petty sum, every instance of corruption results in an unseen consequence. Unfortunately, most of us seem to be satisfied with the visible benefits of the money that we make or the time that we save or the losses that we reduce. Rarely do we go deeper and analyze how corruption is corroding the system and who it affects most, let alone fight it.

The fight against corruption does begin with acknowledging its presence around, but it is not enough only to talk about fighting corruption or merely nod our head in agreement watching television debates. Fighting corruption also cannot be reduced to street-side sloganeering or waving the national flag. It needs to begin with 'us' committing ourselves to staying honest whatever the inconvenience or the price that we need to pay. Resisting the forces that pushes one into indulging an act of corruption is as vital as targeting and punishing those who are corrupt. In the fight against corruption, we must, as a community or society also look at appreciating and valuing the actions of honest people. We need to celebrate goodness and make leading a virtuous life something that we can all be proud about. We have to turn things around and dis-incentivize being corrupt. The price to be paid can indeed be very steep, which is evident from the fact that honest officers have been targeted and some have even lost their lives through machinations of a corrupt system run by a set of corrupt people. Yet, we have to look up to the honest along with looking down upon the corrupt. The reality of corruption hits hard, but can be countered only by hard choices that we as citizens make.

Understanding corruption, and what it takes to fight it

Corruption is often deemed to be one of the greatest impediments to development. Whether it is collusive corruption, where the parties involved are willful participants who collude and short-circuit the system through their corrupt act, or whether it is coercive corruption, where there is a distinct victim, it is the nation's progress that is hindered. And when corruption becomes a systemic issue and begins to be recognized as a cultural rather than a behavioral phenomenon, finding an appropriate response either from the state or its people is that much more complex. While media attention that some of the 'high-profile' scams receive prompts the government to form committees for examining and investigating matters, however needless and ineffective they may be, it is a serious concern that hardly any steps are taken to control the kind of corruption, where relatively small amounts of money or resources are diverted or siphoned off on a regular basis, day after day. Before evolving a response to corruption, it is important to understand what corruption exactly means and gauge how it adversely impacts development.

Corruption, defined as 'the abuse of public power for private gain' (World Bank, 1997), has existed for a long time. It encompasses unilateral abuses by government officials such as embezzlement and nepotism, as well as abuses linking public and private actors such as bribery, extortion, influence peddling, and fraud. India has been ranked 85th in Transparency International's global corruption index in 2014 even as corruption remains one of the key stumbling blocks for the country's progress. Though formal institutional mechanisms of the state exist for fighting corruption, they have not been able to make a significant impact.

Evidence confirms that corruption hurts the poor disproportionately and hinders efforts to achieve the Millennium Development Goals (MDGs) and human development by reducing access to social services and diverting resources away from investments in infrastructure, institutions and social services. Corruption can prevail in both political and bureaucratic offices and can be petty or grand, organized or unorganized. In the political realm, it undermines democracy and good governance by subverting formal processes. Corruption in elections and in legislative bodies reduces accountability and representation in policymaking. Corruption in the judiciary suspends the rule of law, and in public administration, it results in inequity in the provision of services. More generally, it erodes the institutional capacity of the government as procedures are disregarded, resources are siphoned off, and officials are hired or promoted without regard to performance. At the same time, it undermines the legitimacy of government and such democratic values as trust and tolerance. It also undermines economic development by generating considerable distortions and inefficiency.

In the private sector, it increases the cost of business through the practice of illicit payments, the price of negotiating with officials and the risk of breached agreements. Although some claim that corruption reduces costs by cutting red tape, an emerging consensus holds that the availability of bribes induces officials to contrive new rules and delays. Where corruption inflates the cost of business, it also distorts the playing field, shielding firms with the right connections, thereby throttling healthy competition and sustaining inefficient firms. It also generates economic distortions in the public sector by diverting public investment away from social sectors like education and healthcare into capital projects where bribes and kickbacks are more plentiful. Officials may increase the technical complexity of public sector projects to conceal such dealings, thus further distorting investment. It also lowers compliance with construction, environmental, or other regulations, compromises on quality, reduces the controlling and monitoring capabilities of the government and increases budgetary pressures on government. Ultimately, these distortions deter investment and reduce economic growth.

Further, we must also realize that the cost of corruption is not borne by the parties involved alone. It is the people at large who bear the brunt and pay the price in an inefficient and corrupt regime. The impact of corruption, whether it is among the elected representatives or the higher echelons of bureaucracy, in the private sector or the judiciary is seen in how citizens are denied efficient and reliable public services, safety and security, and a guarantee that institutions shall function democratically. It is therefore little surprise that when appropriately triggered, the pent-up frustrations and anger of the common people can take the shape of a popular uprising against corruption.

However, the battle against corruption cannot be won by the energy and passion generated from anger alone. It would take a combination of many elements working synchronously to curb the menace of corruption in our system, if not weed it out effectively. Firstly, we must understand that though corruption is a criminal act, it is rarely a one-time event. The mechanisms to fight corruption must take that into account and people must be prepared to fight as long as it takes. We need to prepare ourselves for the pain of uprooting corruption, as any fight against corruption will necessarily mean sacrifices, sometimes harsh, and we need to brace ourselves to the forces that will prevent any anti-corruption work. The forces need not be actors in the political and administrative arenas alone, but also encompass millions of ordinary citizens who get co-opted as stakeholders into the pecuniary gains that corruption brings.

The backbone of any successful movement against corruption is an enduring political will. There are plenty of examples of how political will at the top has either helped in stemming corrupt practices and resulted in more efficient institutions in the states. Gujarat and Bihar, though not perfect, have made notable strides in this regard. But there are also states like Karnataka that are good examples of how easily corruption can grow and thrive due to the active indulgence of the politicians at the highest level. However, sustaining the political will in the fight against corruption cannot be achieved without constant engagement with the state and pressure from the people at all levels. A corrupt establishment thrives on the knowledge that public memory is short-lived and that it can weather the storm created by sporadic protests of people. This only goes to show that we cannot afford people's pressure on the establishment to slip away.

An unambiguous legal framework that clearly defines bribery, fraud and corruption, with both evidential and procedural provisions is another crucial cog in the wheel. Apart from one's own personal and professional values, the legal dimensions that prevail in a state can deeply influence behavior. We need to be sensitive to the fact that any anti-corruption activity could end up being counterproductive if there is ambiguity in the law. In fact clarity in the law, both in articulation and implementation, is critical in building public confidence and preventing cynicism among people from becoming a deterring factor. While attention must be undeniably paid towards enacting and implementing laws in the right spirit, an aware and socially conscious citizenry is what can provide a campaign against corruption, the ammunition needed to sustain the fight.

In addition to legal frameworks, systems and procedures have to be laid down for enforcement of laws, prevention of corruption and education of citizens. The Karnataka Lokayukta Act is a good example of how much attention needs to be given to this dimension of enforcement and prevention. However, enforcement is an effective deterrent only when the agency has prosecution powers and this lacuna can further contribute to not just making a mockery of the entire agency and the system, but also in eroding public confidence. Further, there is evidence of how poorly defined processes in the law can be interpreted by clever lawyers to the advantage of their clients and used to stifle anti-corruption investigations.

While prevention and enforcement are driven mostly by the state and its agencies, concerted efforts towards mobilizing public support and bringing about attitudinal changes is a critical step in the fight against corruption. People's participation in every step along the way can be instrumental in truly transforming the system to one that not only dis-incentivizes corrupt practices, but also incentivizes the desire to stay honest. It is only large scale citizen engagement that can ensure that being corrupt is not the norm. After all, fighting corruption cannot and should not remain the preserve of a state sponsored agency alone.

When communities affected by corruption and mal-administration get involved, the focus invariably shifts to accountability of the state functionaries. The overall experience of community action through social audit in the Mahatma Gandhi National Rural Employment Guarantee Scheme is quite encouraging and could well be considered as a positive precedence for replicating the concept in other areas. Community support and involvement is a slow process with several obstacles such as non-responsive state mechanisms and political dynamics in its path. But, we cannot expect to root out corruption from the system unless we allow community engagement, and thereby democracy, to grow its roots deep enough.

At an individual level, anti-corruption work is a thankless job and is filled with risks and discomforts. There have been individual crusaders in the government as well as outside of it who have taken it upon themselves to fight the menace and expose themselves to tremendous pressure and dangers, sometimes fatally. As a nation rises in unison against corruption, we must remember and honor these sacrifices and also draw inspiration from them. A well-networked and strategized community movement can help in seeing to it that young lives are not snuffed out by forces detrimental to our nation's true development. Development after all is a multi-layered, multi-dimensional process that must be enduring and inclusive. So is the fight against corruption. Suffice it to say that true development cannot be brought about without a collective battle against corruption.

A nation rises against corruption

Over the last couple of decades and more, stories of corruption and scams have become a common feature in the news both nationally and internationally. In India, corruption scandals of all kinds and scales continue to be reported in the media and the general public has had little respite from either being exposed to stories of corruption or being in situations where one has to indulge in a corrupt act themselves. Whether it was how teachers were recruited in government schools and colleges or how telecom spectrum was allocated, whether it was scams in housing, food-grains, fodder and defense deals or the misappropriations in organizing and hosting international sporting events, our nation has witnessed people of all strata indulge in corrupt practices. The tragedy is that even the most vital government programs and development interventions for the poor such as the Public Distribution System of food grains or the National Rural Health Mission are hit and rendered ineffective by leakages, corruption and misappropriation of funds. Public debate often revolves only around what sound like high value scams. Very rarely does the systematic corruption that results in routine diversion of small amounts of public resources over a long period of time get the attention it deserves. The aggregate of a few rupees systematically siphoned off month after month, year after year in ongoing anti-poverty programs from millions of people does more damage to our system and to the confidence and morale of the ordinary citizenry than perhaps one large scam. People not only begin to feel cynical and hopeless, but also tremendously incapacitated and impotent. They become mere spectators in the scheme of things and generally resign themselves to what is happening. This leaves them powerless and takes away their strength to negotiate and to demand accountability.

Despite the fact that civil society in India has been battling corruption and trying to garner public support from a long time, the issue has seen limited mass support over a sustained period of time. Different approaches have been adopted to tackle corruption and one such approach is to have a stringent law against corruption passed by the Parliament of India. The need for an effective and comprehensive anti-corruption law in the country was felt based on the experiences of many activists who had tried to battle corruption using the Right to Information Act and Prevention of Corruption Act. In 2010, the Government of India had drafted an anti-graft legislation called Lokpal Bill, but it was considered weak and unacceptable by most of civil society despite having included the Prime Minister under the ambit. Many activists, including me subscribed to the view that 'no law' was a better situation than having a 'weak law' and were worried that the government would end up making a law which would not only be ineffective but also make the common man complacent on anti-corruption issues.

It was then that civil society activists across the country got together to draft their own version of the bill and engage the government with this draft. There were different drafts being prepared at the same time including one by the National Campaign for People's Right to Information (NCPRI)[26], which received substantial inputs from Arvind Kejriwal and one by the National Advisory Committee's[27] sub-committee on good governance under the chairmanship of Ms Aruna Roy. Subsequently Arvind also

26 NCPRI started as a campaign in 1996 and was instrumental in drafting the Right to Information Act in India and is today working as an advocacy movement on different issues.

27 National Advisory Council was set up as an advisory body to the Prime Minister during the tenure of the United Progressive Alliance (UPA) Government at the center, in 2004 and was chaired by Ms. Sonia Gandhi through its ten year existence.

came up with another draft around December 2010, as he felt the need for an omnibus act that was strong as well as comprehensive. Around the same time, a few Bengalureans had started a campaign called *Corruption Saaku* (Enough of Corruption!) and during one of the events as part of the campaign, it was decided that the process should be part of a larger civil society initiative and that we needed to get more people on board in our fight for a strong anti-corruption law.

It was indeed Arvind's networking and convincing skills that got a large team on board that included social activist Anna Hazare[28], former Law Minister Shanthi Bhushan, his son and Supreme Court lawyer Prashant Bhushan, former officer of the Indian Police Service Kiran Bedi, social activist and former member of Haryana Legislative Assembly Swami Agnivesh, Justice Santosh Hegde and others to continue the work under the banner of 'India Against Corruption'. Many of us from civil society were convinced that we had to mount an incessant campaign and get the government to consider our points of view while preparing a law. A copy of the early draft was sent to the Prime Minister and to the Chief Ministers of all 28 states. Expectedly, none of them showed any interest in these drafts and we felt completely ignored. As part of our continued advocacy with the government, a few of the activists met with Prime Minister Manmohan Singh on the 7th of March 2011. His lukewarm response left us with no doubt that the government was not serious about bringing a strong and effective anti-corruption law.

It was then that Anna Hazare in an emotional response announced that he would go on an indefinite hunger-fast till the nation hears a firm commitment by the government to pass the

28 Kiran Baburao Hazare, popularly known as Anna Hazare is an Indian social activist from the state of Maharashtra who has led several movements towards rural development and campaigns against corruption within the state and the national level. A man inspired by the ideals of Mahatma Gandhi and Swami Vivekananda, Anna Hazare rose to prominence as the face of the anti-corruption protests in 2011 and 2012 undertaken by thousands of people across India in various cities.

Jan Lokpal Bill[29]. None of us were prepared for this and the next few days revealed that the government was also taken aback at the national awakening that was churned. The media swung into action and projected the fast and the campaign for the Jan Lokpal Bill prominently for weeks to come; primetime news was dominated by debates and discussions on the issue. Prominent social activists also joined the struggle and while political parties wanted to utilize the situation to their advantage, Anna Hazare was steadfast in his refusal to allow any politician to sit with him.

What was unprecedented was the support that Anna's fast received from ordinary people across the country. Rallying to the call of Anna, people of different ages and walks of life spilled on to the streets and began demanding the Jan Lokpal Bill. The spontaneous response of the people was a clear indication of how the citizens of the country were fed up with the corruption that hurts them on a daily basis. The government buckled, owing to the massive public sentiment against them and agreed to table the bill in the forthcoming Parliamentary Session and to forming a Joint Drafting Committee. Anna, the anti-corruption crusader, who was on fast for 98 hours by then, agreed to call off his fast with the condition that a strong anti-corruption bill must be passed by 15th of August 2011, failing which he would agitate again.

In the months that followed, parleys were held with the government and the Joint Drafting Committee had a few sittings. However, the committee could not come to a consensus on several terms and in August 2011, the government introduced its own version of the bill in the Parliament. The entire handling of the working of the committee came under criticism from civil society as well as political parties. The team that was spearheading the campaign was left unsatisfied with the version that was introduced in the Parliament

29 Jan Lokpal Bill or Citizen's Ombudsman Act is a bill drafted by civil society activists in India that aims to tackle corruption in public offices. The bill sought the appointment of an independent body (called Jan Lokpal) to investigate cases of corruption. (See glossary)

and true to his word Anna Hazare prepared himself to undertake another fast in Delhi from the 16th of August.

What followed was another evidence of the government's poor reading of the mood of the people when it undertook the misadventure of arresting Anna Hazare. People's sentiments against the government across the country were heightened to a new level after this move and India witnessed an unprecedented show of support from its citizens, the young, especially in solidarity with the battle against corruption. Never before had collective actions against corruption been seen in such quick succession. Despite its shortcomings, the movement had clearly touched a new generation as could be seen by the way the youth had responded. The question however is whether the experience has left an imprint on their minds to commit to the cause of the nation's progress. The spontaneity seen in the movement masks questions about how well the people who demanded Jan Lokpal Bill understood its provisions or the differences between the various versions, or for that matter about people's awareness of the levels of corruption in public offices around them and their plans, if any, to undertake long-term action locally.

Nevertheless, it marked a new uprising in India and this indicated hope. In the long, arduous battle against corruption, hope is an invaluable ally.

From the streets of Mysuru

A day after India celebrated its 64th Independence Day, news broke out that the veteran crusader against corruption, Anna Hazare was arrested by the police and no reason was given for this action. A few reports came in that he had been placed under preventive custody, but what was clear was that the government had bungled its response to the hunger strike that Anna was due to begin. Along with him, at least two hundred and fifty other campaigners against corruption were also detained and it was widely felt that the crackdown bore resemblances to the crackdown of the mid-seventies when a state of Emergency was declared in India during the tenure of the then Prime Minister, Indira Gandhi. The circumstances were certainly different, but the actions of the government seemed to have reached similar overreaching proportions, and the right to peaceful protest was being trampled by a state unwilling to provide space for dissent and disagreement.

The entire nation was closely following the developments leading to the arrest of Anna Hazare. It was only about four months since Government of India had accepted the demand for a legislation against graft and set in motion a process for drafting the bill following a hunger strike led by Hazare and supported by many anti-corruption activists with protests in different cities across India. A draft of the Lokpal Bill was approved by the Union Cabinet towards the end of July 2011, but this draft fell short of the expectations of the anti-corruption movement and was criticized as a weak bill as it left certain provisions such as bringing the Prime Minister, the Central Bureau of Investigation and Judiciary out of its purview. Anna Hazare had announced that he will agitate by going on a fast on the 16th of August 2011 to press his demand for a stronger legislation against corruption in public offices.

The arrest triggered instant protests across India and tens of thousands of people took to the streets. Back in Mysuru, we decided to take our campaign against corruption forward and gave a call for all like-minded individuals and progressive institutions to lay aside any individual labels and come together for this fight against corruption and fight for a strong Lokpal bill. The incidents in Delhi had definitely touched a chord among people, evident from the encouraging turnout despite the heavy downpour in Mysuru at that time. Hundreds of people, young and old, students and retirees, joined together to express their concern. Together, it was decided to take the campaign forward under the banner of Mysore Against Corruption and that all ideologies except that of fighting corruption would be kept aside from this platform. It was also decided that the 'Satyagraha'[30] would be carried on under the statue of Mahatma Gandhi located at Gandhi Square near the city's Town Hall. Along with the public protest, there were plans for many other micro-events in the suburbs of the city to get students and other citizens involved.

The streets of Mysuru resonated with the prevailing mood of citizens on the streets across the country at the time. It was a kind of citizen engagement the country had not seen for a long time, when people who normally stayed a safe distance from protests were challenging the establishment. It was also a ripe opportunity for political parties to exploit the situation for their gains. As a collective, it was something we had to guard against and when a major national political party tried to gate-crash at the protest site, the

---

30 Satyagraha is a form of protest or non-violent struggle based on principles of truthfulness. The word translates to insistence on truth and was made popular by Mahatma Gandhi during India's struggle for independence.

citizens' resolve was put to test. The party was politely turned away, while its members were welcomed to join the protest as individuals.

Yet, this did not mean that we were closed to the idea of engaging with the political class. The campaign against corruption is inherently political. We had the Member of Parliament from the Mysuru Parliamentary constituency, who belonged to the party in power at the center then, visit us and share his views on the Lokpal Bill and the arrest of Anna Hazare. We had reached out to him and wanted him to hear us and carry our thoughts and emotions on these issues to his party and colleagues in the Parliament. Though we never expected him to turn up, he did come and even agreed that the arrest of Anna was not an appropriate response of his government. He shared his view that each person had his own way of expressing dissent and as long as it was within the purview of law, the state could not and should not suppress it. He also agreed to be a representative of the people and take our views to Parliament on the need for a strong Lokpal Bill.

For six days from that day, we the citizens of Mysuru gathered every day in solidarity with the movement against corruption that the nation as a whole was witnessing. This included fasts, candle-light vigils and marches, rallies taken out on motorcycles across the city, music and sloganeering, and spreading awareness among people in public places about the Lokpal Bill and the specific clauses that were found wanting in the version presented in the Parliament. The passion and the energy that the students from various schools and colleges brought to the campaign was unparalleled. Numbering in thousands, they indeed helped spread an infectious enthusiasm, while people from different backgrounds and walks of life supported the city's campaign in their own ways.

Starting from a local *shamiana* (tent shelter) provider, who put up a waterproof structure at the protest venue at his own expense, other local merchants and the taxi drivers' association, who ensured a steady supply of drinking water, bananas and guavas, it was a protest backed by common people right from the first day. On the second day, representatives of the auto drivers association, the chemists and druggists association and the youth group of the Jain community dropped in. Over the next couple of days we were joined by many other organizations and groups including an association of the physically challenged, members of a local ladies club, different student groups and NGOs. We had doctors from the Indian Medical Association, the Mysuru Clinical Society, the Family Physicians Association, Association of Physicians of India and the Mysuru Medical College Alumni Association come and participate in the protest. The campaign had managed to touch individuals and collectives, many of whom had taken to the streets for the first time, indicating how everyone was affected by corruption. We also had the former Speaker of the Karnataka Assembly come in and pledge his support to the campaign.

The Rotary Club had organized a candle light vigil in the evening in which businessmen, government officials, children, and young people walked together, braving the rain. The police, for their part, were very polite and managed the situation quite well despite the numbers swelling into thousands. In the information age, the media plays a role like no other and can make or break campaigns and resistances such as this. The media had been generally supportive of the campaign throughout the country and Mysuru was no different.

The students and youth were of course the lifeblood of all that was taking place. On the second day itself, an estimated six thousand students from different colleges marched towards Gandhi Square shouting slogans. School children from a popular local school also participated. The atmosphere was so charged up with groups singing patriotic songs and shouting '*Vande Mataram*' and '*Bharat Mata ki Jai*'[31] spontaneously. While engineering students helped in setting up a blog and a Facebook page for the campaign, students of CAVA (Chamarajendra Academy of Visual Arts), a fine-arts school

31 Bharat Mata Ki Jai and Vande Mataram are nationalist slogans translating to Victory to Mother India and Salute to Mother

based in the city, led by one of their alumni decided to have a live painting demonstration on the issue. Three of their colleagues also had different anti-corruption messages painted all over their bodies.

On the third day of the campaign, I received a call from a young student of one of the colleges in the city informing me that all the students from her college wanted to join the protest, but their college authorities were not very keen about this. The students had decided to stay out of their classes if they were not allowed to take to the streets. I visited the college and spoke to them about the Bill and the need to keep the flame of the protest burning while at the same time ensuring that their studies would not be compromised. The college authorities were also very happy to extend their support and promised to come with all their students, numbering in thousands, in support of the campaign. It was indeed a great joy to see young girls, mostly aged between eighteen and twenty, passionately committed to fighting corruption in India. To this day, I hope that the experience of participating in this campaign has left a permanent imprint on the minds of these students to lead a career and a life of honesty and refuse to succumb to corruption.

On the fifth day, the students and youth volunteers had organized a bike rally for awareness building. About 200 young people were expected to ride around the suburbs of Mysuru city and talk to people about the campaign, its demands and the differences in the versions of the anti-graft bills. The grounds of a centrally located school close to the University of Mysuru was the starting point of the rally. Within an hour, we saw the grounds of the school become a surging mass of young people with their motorcycles and scooters. Young men and women came in thousands and soon we had over a thousand bikes assembled. We started off on the rally through the main thoroughfares of the city and traveled through most of the residential and commercial locations. Volunteers who rode pillion stepped off to distribute pamphlets, apply stickers bearing anti-corruption messages on vehicles and to talk to people about the

Bill. The noise of their two wheelers and the blaring of the horns added to the energy and enthusiasm. One could get a taste of the difficulty in managing emotional campaigns, especially involving highly charged up young people. It was indeed a great achievement that all across the nation, the struggle had been nonviolent and peaceful.

We had decided to end the campaign on the sixth day and the day being a Sunday, we had the largest gathering we'd had. The highlight of the morning session was the music played by *Rock Vrunda*, a rock band made up of engineering students and fresh graduates. They not only kept the audience engaged with their fusion music but were also the cynosure of the media. Though there were requests to continue the protest, we had to explain that the battle against corruption is a long drawn-out one, which would require a different kind of leadership and vision. I had spoken the previous day on how we need to keep up the momentum and go beyond our demand for a bill and continue our movement to bring in a corruption-free Mysuru district. It was important that the enormous positive energy generated be channelized into something meaningful and constructive. The time had come to move beyond a mere event and take it further as a sustained movement against corruption. We now needed to create a platform that would provide information, support and sustenance to this struggle and help mobilize sincere and committed citizens to fight for good governance.

The political dimensions of the campaign

The entire campaign against corruption in India marked by the series of protests in the years 2011 and 2012 offer important lessons for us as citizens demanding a corruption-free nation and society. The campaign had seen an unprecedented level of participation from people who had rarely taken to the streets in protest. However, the campaign itself had gone through a cycle of enchantment and disenchantment in the minds of the public in the subsequent months. On the third of August 2012, Anna Hazare and his team called off their indefinite fast that was organized for voicing inaction of the government on allegations of corruption against several of its ministers. The fast was called off ten days after it had started and it had accompanied an announcement that they would discontinue their talks with the government and also that there would be no more protests under the purported banner of 'Team Anna'. Coinciding with the end of the protest, a new political outfit was formed and the battle against corruption was set to take on an altogether new dimension.

Understandably, such a decision evoked mixed responses from people around the country. Though the announcement at that time was sudden, the events of the preceding six to eight months indicated that it was part of a larger, but seemingly misdirected strategy and unfortunately not based on consensus. It was a decision that needed more careful analysis, before one could draw conclusions.

My own thoughts were that it was something the movement was not ready for and thus I had my reservations about it, while also being cautiously optimistic.

The country had seen many a relevant social movement fizzle out once it turned political. In our own backyard in Karnataka, we had two extraordinary movements that had given voice to thousands of marginalized people. Both the Dalit movement of the 1970s and the farmers' movement that began in 1980 envisaged changes, which the mainstream society was not ready to comprehend and acknowledge. Despite this, both movements gathered incredible momentum and established themselves as the voices of the people they represented. However, what began as a 'social response' to the issues for vulnerable communities and farmers, with the support of large numbers of ordinary people, gradually got politicized and lost much of its sheen.

The context of these movements was indeed different from the 'anti-corruption' struggle. Yet, we need to place in perspective the ground support that the anti-corruption movement got in its early days. A large number of ordinary citizens, disillusioned with the system, jumped on the bandwagon with an expectation that Anna would wave his magic wand and would change things overnight. Many of them were impatient, young, urban, middle-class people with little understanding of social processes, expecting that the system would respond to the 'visible' pressure that they were creating. For a weary nation looking for the 'magic pill', Anna provided the ideal stage for one to express ones frustrations and build hopes of a better tomorrow. Little did people realize that emotional campaigns are difficult to sustain and a 'system' enmeshed with the desire to maintain status-quo would not let go that easily. The movement also did not engage many rural, vulnerable and marginalized communities who constitute the major portion of the silent and voiceless victims of the corruption that is prevalent in India.

The media's engagement with the movement was proportional

to the extent their readers and viewers engaged with the struggle. With their constituents losing interest, the media too moved away from the continuous coverage they gave to the struggle in the initial weeks. It is a moot point whether the media aroused the masses or the aroused masses gave a reason for the media to engage in this movement. The reality is that when the visibility of the campaign was lowered, the issue of fighting corruption relegated itself from mainstream public discourse.

The government at the time, with its share of seasoned politicians responded exactly as predicted. Though all politicians may not be corrupt, most of the ones I have interacted with, concede that one cannot survive in electoral politics by playing straight. The political class comprised experienced men and women who knew that the best way to fight this movement was to wear the opponents down. By constantly resorting to the line that the Parliament, and not the streets, is the space where laws are framed, it seemed that several leaders of the movement, namely Arvind Kejriwal and the father-son duo of Shanthi and Prashant Bhushan were nudged into the realm of electoral politics, and into believing that the battle against corruption should ensue in that sphere. The political class had played the script to perfection. Party politics and electoral politics was their home ground and they threw the bait to their detractors, the key members of Team Anna. Not only was the bait taken, but Team Anna was also effectively disbanded.

Not that electoral politics should be an untouchable affair. The biggest concern at the time was the realization that team members who did take the route of electoral politics did not have the Machiavellian abilities to think and act like 'politicians'. Even the capability to manage the politics that had crept into the movement seemed absent. The skill sets that make an enduring politician in order to take this battle to the turf of much-seasoned campaigners needed to be built. Social mobilization could take them only to a point, and politics was a different ball game altogether, which required shrewdness and acumen to understand and capitalize on people's aspirations, build a financial base and willingness to be accommodative. All of this could eventually evolve in the long run, but at that time, it seemed that the politicians had a clear edge given the asymmetry of resources needed, and available to fight the political battle, and the fact that they could do it on their own terms. For all the people's mobilization that had shaped over the year or so, it seemed that the leaders of the anti-corruption campaign would be defeated electorally in a bid to push them into irrelevance.

But then, this was also an opportunity to bring a new paradigm into Indian politics. A new wave of clean politics could be ushered in with the citizens being more demanding of the candidates who represent them. Maybe elections could be contested and won based on people's issues rather on the back of money and muscle power. There were a handful of reasons to be hopeful, but the risks seemed to outnumber them. The bigger danger was that this defeat would not be of just the handful of brave people or of the hundreds of activists across the country. A defeat could have a catastrophic effect on all social movements and would be an ominous sign to activists fighting many a successful battle. Importantly, the class of people that engaged in the campaign against corruption mostly had a negative attitude towards politics and it could be a damaging setback. The painstakingly built campaign that had aroused the passion and imagination of the common man was falling apart. At the same time, the drawbacks of the campaign, which included the inability to reach out to the most marginalized and vulnerable populations stood out.

The risks indeed seemed too many to fathom, not least of which was that the anti-corruption plank itself was perceived to have been compromised. It was unimaginable that any new political outfit arising out of the movement would have the resources to match the millions of rupees their rivals spent on each election. There were naturally a few who opted out of the transition as they saw all politicians as corrupt and were inclined to paint the members of the new political party too with the same brush. My own feeling was that they would have better served the cause by engaging with activists and organizations across the country. Instead of spewing venom on all politicians and political parties, they should have tried to engage with the good people in the system and build a coalition that would have stood by them at a later date. Engaging with the legislative arm of the state did not necessarily mean 'entering' Parliament. In any case, no party could hope to pass a strong Lokpal Bill, the key demand of the campaign, without enough seats in either houses of the Parliament.

There was a danger of not only becoming a laughing-stock, but of setting the movement behind by several years, if not decades. The team could have strategized and spent time building strong citizens' groups to exert pressure on the political system, which could have resulted in a semblance of accountability and transparency in the 2014 elections. It would have provided a logical culmination to the movement against corruption, one that would have focused on restoring people's faith in democratic and constitutional processes.

Post the anti-corruption movement of 2011 and 2012, the turn of events was quite remarkable. Aam Admi Party (AAP), the political outfit took birth on 26th of November 2012, the 63rd anniversary of the day the Constitution of India was adopted. Led by Arvind Kejriwal, the party contested the Delhi Assembly Elections in 2013, met with unprecedented success for a party making its debut, and was in power for 49 turbulent days, though the party had not gained a clear majority. The party then set its eyes on the Lok Sabha elections of 2014, in which most of its candidates suffered heavy defeats, except for four who were victorious. The party contested the Delhi Assembly Elections again and exceeded expectations by garnering 67 out of 70 seats. It seemed that a novel method of winning elections had been established, but only time will tell if the party can deliver on the mandate of providing stable and good governance and also sustain the respect and faith of the people in the long run. After forming the government in Delhi, infighting within the party and controversies have exposed fault lines and what appears like dictatorial tendencies of the key protagonists indicates that the rise of alternative politics espoused by the party may be short lived, even as its ethos seems to have become a casualty of power politics. In a bid to seize political power, the party also seems to have erred in its choice of members and many people with questionable antecedents are now elected members of the Delhi Assembly. It is natural to feel concerned that this party may not turn out to be very different from the other political outfits in the country. An anxious nation continues to keep watch.

"THERE CAN BE NO DAILY DEMOCRACY,
WITHOUT DAILY CITIZENSHIP"

RALPH NADER

Citizen engagement towards making democracy work

Democracy is every citizen's business. Making participatory democracy work is in the hands of citizens, and exercising their electoral franchise is the first step towards this. A 'vote' in the world's largest democracy is however a complex phenomenon given how it is sought, and how people respond to it. The Indian electorate is known to be an intelligent one, but the factors influencing them, if election campaigns are anything to go by, are rarely issues of development. Money, material, muscle, lineage, caste, religion and crime often constitute a potpourri of factors that play a role in the electoral fortunes of people. It is an unhealthy trend that we collectively ought to put an end to. By voting responsibly, by being politically more conscious, by demanding accountability, by participating, by resisting, or in other words by making democracy work.

This section captures experiences and reflections of having engaged with citizens towards ensuring greater and responsible participation in the electoral processes before and during elections at different levels. In 2013 and 2014, these efforts took shape of a formal campaign in and around Mysuru, but received recognition and appreciation in forums across the country.

What is the will of the people?

Between 2004 and 2013, the state of Karnataka had witnessed enormous political turmoil. The single largest political party that had emerged from the 2004 Assembly Elections was kept out of power by a coalition of other parties that formed the government. In the middle of its term, one of the partners of the coalition broke away to join hands with the other larger party and stake claim to form the government, and this arrangement broke again due to political differences. Political bickering reached a nadir by the time the state went into elections again in 2008. Following this, there was a party at the helm of the state which ruled for five years, but its tenure was marred with controversies, corruption, revolts and an unbridled hunger among politicians for power.

In the thick of the political games being played, it seemed that the people in power hardly remembered that they were representing people who had voted for them. As citizens, we wondered if the representative democracy we were experiencing was worse than no democracy at all. We were asking ourselves the basic question – what is the will of the people, and whether it has any relevance at all? Are we as citizens, merely instruments meant to elect our representatives and subsequently move away to the background? Or should we take on more proactive and sustained roles in ensuring that these elected representatives continue to serve our interests, instead of their own?

Based on our own understanding of the political parties and their stated manifestos, we elect our representatives either as members to the Legislative Assembly (MLA) of the state or to the Parliament of India (MP) and expect them to further the interests of the electorate. It is an unstated commitment from the elected member to not only represent the majority whose votes brought them power, but also to serve everyone within their constituency without distinction. They are not expected to sell out their interests to the highest bidder, ignoring the interests of the people that they represent.

But then, one also wonders why they wouldn't do so. We did see most of them spend unbelievably huge sums of money to get elected. I have personally witnessed the buying of votes and loyalties both in rural and urban areas. When democracy comes so cheap and votes can simply be bought in the electoral marketplace, how can citizens turn around and question what these MLAs have done? During a particularly volatile political situation in the state in early 2009, it was rumored that each MLA was bribed huge sums of money and offered positions of power to either stay within the party's fold, switch allegiance and cross-vote or to simply resign from the assembly itself. The nation witnessed embarrassing scenes when opposition party members waved wads of cash in the Indian Parliament during a crucial confidence vote for the central government in 2008. In such a scenario, it is difficult even to fathom whether 'democracy' can be rescued from the jaws of power-hungry leaders and a corrupted, indifferent citizenry. When the path of reaching positions of power itself is riddled with corruption, how can we expect either the citizens or their elected leaders to behave differently when in power?

The pity is that on one side we have a silent group of people, mostly middle class and literate who consider that ignoring the political process and elections is the best way to cope with rampant electoral corruption, while on the other side, we have a large number of people who increasingly have started to believe that they need to 'cash in' on the situation and have become willing participants in corrupting the entire democratic process. How do we navigate through a difficult but much-needed change process in not just educating the people who contest elections, but also the people who vote for them? How does one bring together like-minded people who are sitting on the fence, get them to shed their inertia, tear through their middle class veneer and participate in this process of change? Would it be possible to usher in a political process based on ethical considerations, true democratic principles (both within and outside a political party) and a genuine desire to serve the citizenry, one which is not driven by money, caste and a senseless desire to stay in power forever? How do we eliminate the barriers of entry to the political arena and make it feasible for well-meaning people to give it a shot? Can we look at creating such a force by bringing together such people who can throw away their own individual ego needs and coalesce to form a critical mass, large enough to get the ball rolling?

These were questions that were to eventually inspire an intensive campaign launched by SVYM that engaged with the people of Mysuru and part of Kodagu districts of Karnataka. Entitled 'Making Democracy Work', the campaign received financial support from a non-governmental organization committed to bringing transparency in the electoral processes in India along with reforms such as reduction of money power and participation of candidates with criminal charges, among others. The messages of the campaign were simple, like "NO NOTE FOR MY VOTE" but profound in terms of the meaning they carried in the context of elections and the charged atmosphere that it generates. We also had the confidence to reach a large number of people with our message because of our belief that the will of the people could make a difference. The disappointment with the system, the complaints, the frustrations and a sense of helplessness among people at large had to be read as indications that people cared and all that was needed was to convert that negative energy to a constructive expression in the electoral process. It was a belief in democracy itself.

If we trace democracy back to its roots, we discover that neither its appearance nor its survival is inevitable. A democratic community can survive if its citizens see participation in the political process as a duty as well as a responsibility. The strength of Indian society is its resilience and ability to bounce back from adverse situations. The will to lead better lives, the will to work hard, the will to engage in development, the desire to see a thriving nation and the belief in each other has always been there. All that we need to do is ensure that this will is reflected in the democratic processes that determine the kind of government we get and the kind of country we will live in.

The onus is on the voter

In March 2013, elections to the Urban Local Bodies (City Municipal Corporations) in the state of Karnataka were held. The Mysuru City Corporation elections were a closely contested affair and had their fair share of drama. Campaigning for the elections was not as noisy as before and did not end up defacing the city with flex hoardings all around, thanks to new rules and restrictions on campaigning. There were more door-to-door campaigns and people moved around in large groups canvassing for their candidates.

I met one such group and was talking to one of the ladies who was part of the canvassing team. While she knew the name of the candidate, I found it amusing that she did not know the party that he belonged to. Feeling curious, I started probing deeper, only to realize that most of the people in the group had been hired on a daily basis for the purpose of canvassing. She told me that she earned her living by working as a domestic helper in a couple of houses. The week gone by had been very profitable for her. She was being given a thousand rupees and three square meals every day. All she had to do was show up and be part of this group and walk around the whole day between 9 am and 6 pm. For her, elections meant an opportunity to earn a little extra money and she was very happy that the elections to the Legislative Assembly of the state were rapidly approaching. Her only grouse was that the men were being paid five hundred rupees more than the women.

I continued to follow up the electoral fortunes of this candidate who actually ended up winning. As part of his victory celebrations, he distributed set-top-boxes to all families in his ward. No one could now say that elections had not benefited his local constituency. Interacting with a couple of families in his ward, I realized that many of them were given at least five hundred rupees to come out and vote on the polling day. The voters were indeed happy as most of the candidates, including the losing ones, had ended up paying money for their votes. It was indeed funny that despite putting up his vote for sale, the average citizen still ended choosing and casting his vote for the person he wanted. Can this be construed as a semblance of democracy at work, albeit in a perverted way? Could the voter who accepted a bribe and yet voted as per his own will, consider himself incorruptible and feel happy about it?

An interaction with one of the candidates who contested the elections revealed another side of the story. He explained to me that it was indeed easy to criticize the politicians for bribing the voters. He asked me why nobody spoke much about the 'corrupt voter'. Politicians and political parties would only be happy to spend less on the elections, he argued, but spending on the voter was essential to stay in the game. For him paying the voter may not guarantee a victory, but not doing so virtually guaranteed a defeat. People like him did not want to take any chances and had joined the bandwagon of giving out money and freebies in order to be in the race.

It is tough to put a finger on who started the mess of voter-bribing that we see today – political parties or the people. It is clear however that it cannot thrive without the partaking of both. We have let this corruption reach such proportions that any honest person is driven to despair. It shouldn't be hard to realize that our rights as citizens and the responsibilities that accompany our citizenship should not be for sale. Selling them would only weaken our democracy and make good governance the immediate casualty.

It is pertinent to note that while we as citizens decry politicians and administrators as being corrupt, the same is the view held by the other side about us. My conversation with the aforementioned candidate clearly indicates so. Would it be a surprise if he might be laughing in private every time somebody called him corrupt? Wouldn't he then be an apt representative of a corrupt voter? Aren't we ourselves responsible for the decay and degeneration that we see in our governments and administration? We can hardly blame our politicians and the bureaucracy alone for the lack of progress and development.

Representative democracy allows us to express our political power only through our representatives and this prevents citizens from realizing how their non-participation can result in a weakening of our democratic institutions. We, as common citizens, have to go beyond this, enlarge the scope of our engagement and bring about 'Participatory Democracy' in the real sense of the term. We need to understand that elections are only one facet of our responsibility and we need to continue to engage with the people we have elected to office even after the elections. Only when we begin doing this, can we enforce accountability and give the much-needed life back to democracy.

The Democracy Index 2011 shows India as a 'Flawed Democracy' indicating that we have a lot of ground to cover before we can aspire to make it to the list of 'Full Democracies'. We cannot be satisfied with the mere claim that we are the largest democracy in the world. We also need to move towards becoming a fully functional and a healthy one with citizens being aware of their rights and consciously performing their duties too. It can begin by shedding the image of the corrupt voter – from the minds of the politicians and from our own minds. With several factors like religion, caste, population size, criminalization, cronyism, poverty and regional differences that affect the working of our democracy, we need to realize that strengthening our fledgling democracy through active participation is the only real solution that can work. We as citizens have to commit ourselves to practicing transparency in all our dealings, hold ourselves to the highest standards of account-ability and unhesitatingly participate in all matters concerning our development. Only when we do that, will we gain the moral right to question our elected representatives and hold them accountable. Citizenship does demand a price and unless we pay it willingly and intentionally, we cannot hope to change our nation's course for the better. Responsible citizenship today can also positively influence the voters of an upcoming generation. The onus indeed is on all of us.

Making Democracy Work – The premise

"Why are you asking me to forgo the pressure cooker or the mixer-grinder (blender) that I will get?"

This was a question a middle-class homemaker asked our team that was carrying out a door-to-door campaign trying to reach out to the people and urge them to vote responsibly and refrain from being influenced by 'bribes' offered by candidates contesting in the elections. Our team faced many other questions as well and at times, it was quite a challenging experience to find responses to such questions in a way that could be reasoned with those who posed them. We had decided early in our campaign that our focus would be on the issue of voter-bribing and responsible voting. All our communication tools and methods would have this as the central message, while being cognizant about various other issues surrounding the election process. This door-to-door campaign was one of the many methods deployed to reach out to citizens with the aim of reducing electoral corruption carried out weeks before the elections to the Legislative Assembly of Karnataka in 2013.

Among the plethora of issues surrounding electoral processes in India, why did ridding the election from distribution of free-bies to voters matter so much? Why, when massive scandals and power-broking were being unearthed, was a campaign asking voters to refrain from petty bribes and look at the background and the knowledge of the candidate? The results of an analysis[32] of 62,847 candidates who had contested either Parliamentary or State Assembly elections since 2004 throws some answers. Among many noteworthy points, the analysis highlights that the factors aiding an electoral victory is a combination of criminal background and amount of wealth one possesses – not stances on issues of development, not progressive reforms, and not democratic ideals.

There was a 23% chance of winning if the candidate had a criminal background, and 30% of the Members of Lok Sabha (the Lower House of the Indian Parliament) at that time were facing criminal charges. All the political parties without exception had given tickets to candidates who had declared that there were pending criminal cases against them. In addition to having criminal charges, the amount of wealth that one owned also was a vital factor. The average assets of 8,790 candidates who were elected either as Members of Parliament or as Members of Legislative Assemblies of different states was worth 38.3 million rupees among those who won. Those who finished second in the race had average assets worth 24.7 million rupees. The average assets of those with criminal background was 43.1 million rupees. The analysis also showed an average increase of 134% in declared wealth in less than five years of candidates who were going to contest the elections again.

These numbers clearly indicate that the chances of winning an election in India are higher if one has money or a criminal background. Does democracy need a bigger threat than this? This is also a threat to the sanctity of the Constitution of India which we gave unto ourselves. The preamble that pronounces **EQUALITY of status and of opportunity**, and promotion of **FRATERNITY assuring the dignity of the individual and the unity and integrity of the Nation,** is violated if we let money and power prevent

32 The analysis was carried out in 2013 by Association for Democratic Reforms, a non-profit organization working on electoral reforms towards bringing accountability and transparency in the election process and towards reducing the influence of money power in elections

well-intentioned and transparent citizens from contesting the elections. The continuing of such trends would mean that the gulf between ordinary citizens and those in power would only increase over time. How would an elected 'representative' then ever understand what grassroots perspectives are and pave way for development that matters to the people?

Our attempts to engage with people on corruption and the influence of money in elections was centered on being able to relate to this question. That was the premise of the 'Making Democracy Work' campaign undertaken in Mysuru and part of Kodagu districts of Karnataka, wherein we reached out to hundreds of thousands of people through a variety of activities including talks, rallies, events in public places, door-to-door campaigns, street-plays, posters and articles in the media among others.

The roles played by the Election Commission, the police and courts are important in ensuring that elections and all the activities in the run-up to the elections are conducted legally and in accordance with democratic principles, but they have their limitations. People, or the electorate must be earnest and willing to comply with the guidelines set by the Election Commission and other agencies. That can only happen when people refuse to be influenced by money, caste, threats or any other kind of coercion from candidates or their political parties in order to get votes. In fact, people must go one step further and begin to question the candidates on their manifestos, their development agenda, awareness of local issues and their basic knowledge about the Constitution. That was what the Making Democracy Work campaign encouraged people to do.

More often than not, people's responses were positive. They saw that if they refused the money, pressure-cooker, mixer grinder, alcohol, or other freebies offered by the contesting candidates, they would retain the moral right to question their representative on development action that really matters. This would not have been possible without the campaign team themselves being convinced about the message. It was through a combination of training, experience and self-reflection that the team members rose above being mere messengers of a campaign, but advocates of democracy itself. That conviction about the premise of the campaign was one of the strengths as well as one of the more enduring successes of 'Making Democracy Work'.

A people's view of free and fair elections

Personally, the 'Making Democracy Work' campaign was very educative for me. I had the opportunity to travel around the entire district of Mysuru and meet young people, students, members of self-help groups, farmers, software engineers, factory workers and housewives. We wanted to reach out to every citizen and get them to participate responsibly in the elections and make democracy work. We saw mixed reactions from people. There was hope, aspiration, demand for change, a feeling of helplessness and sometimes a resigned acceptance of the morass to which our political set-up had sunk. The kind of questions that people asked reflected the hopes and aspirations of the common man. The despair and frustration born out of the helplessness in people, the inability to change, the corruption and indifference both in the voters and in the candidates were all palpable. Many of them questioned us on the impossibility of the task that we had taken upon ourselves. They wanted to know if free and fair elections could ever be a reality in our country. The newspapers were reporting the different steps that the Election Commission was taking in order to do this, but somehow the people did not seem convinced.

I started asking people what they thought would contribute to free and fair elections from their perspective. The answers I got were very informative and showed that not only does the common man notice and perceive such things, he also has his own metric to measure free and fair elections. Importantly, it indicated that even beneath the indifferent or apathetic exterior expression, a common citizen still craved progress and was driven by hope. Perhaps the negative expressions are just a result of frustrations of not witnessing a clean and accountable political system, which they aspire for from within. In the conversations, they revealed the numerous ways in which people were being lured during elections, but had no hesitations in separating right from wrong.

In one village, some people told me how non-vegetarian dinners were being provided regularly for flimsy reasons. They asked how people who hardly knew anyone in their village would find a reason to throw a party and feed them all. Another group of young people told me how every village now suddenly had a cricket team. All young boys not only got bats, balls and wickets to play, but also tee-shirts and caps. They also found sponsors for their games and prizes. They only wanted to know how and why everyone except the district authorities knew who their sponsors were.

Speaking to a few shop owners dealing with consumer durables gave me an understanding how their sales spiked during election months. Voters were given gift coupons and vouchers that they could exchange for consumer goods once the elections were over. Cleverly, it was ensured that these coupons were valid only after the elections were over and the code of conduct no longer applied. Discussions with women almost always brought out the issue of easy and free availability of liquor during elections. They wanted to know how despite the measures claimed by the district authorities, so much liquor was available in the run up to the elections.

Election time is also an opportunity for people to earn a livelihood. They get paid for mobilizing people, for accompanying the candidate while filing nomination, while they canvass, and to man the booths. One candidate from a national party told me that people had to be paid to come and celebrate their victories too.

There are prescribed limits to how many vehicles can be used for election campaigns as well as a limit on the fuel consumed, which is supposed to be monitored by the authorities. However, people are skeptical about whether these procedures work as local taxis are always difficult to get during election time. One taxi owner told me that this was the best month for him and that his vehicle was booked for the whole month by a person completely unknown to him. All that he cared about was the fact that he got paid by the day though he levied charges that were more than one and a half times the normal tariff.

All these were in addition to the numerous stories of cash, liquor, sarees and other freebies distributed during elections that we would hear almost every day. And when people shared these bits of information, they always had accompanying questions: Why couldn't a ban on liquor be strictly enforced or why couldn't the government monitor the disbursal of unusually high numbers of gift coupons and vouchers? Why couldn't gatherings of people be restricted or why the dinners could not be monitored? These questions indicated the innate desire among people for elections to be contested fairly. A set of elderly middle-class men opined that it was a sense of impunity that ruled the roost among individuals and political parties. They felt that unless visible and timely penal action against electoral malpractices was taken, the offenders would not fear breaking the law.

My interactions with many former and the then Chief Election Commissioner had left no doubt in my mind that they were all trying to ensure free and fair elections. All of them have been trying to bring in different processes to clean up the system and conduct the elections transparently and efficiently. They are indeed doing their bit especially in cleaning up and updating electoral rolls, which itself is a gigantic exercise along with monitoring of the entire process. The Election Commission of India has over the years introduced many reforms and innovations including the introduction of Electronic Voting Machines, the concept of a model code of conduct, the photo identity cards, and it keeps upgrading rules and procedures to keep up with the changing times, but largely remains unacknowledged by the general public for its efforts. The Commission also faces innumerable hurdles and challenges, thanks to the frenzied atmosphere that elections generate, but they deserve much credit in choreographing the world's largest dance of democracy, the General Elections of India.

People's vision of free and fair elections however cannot be achieved by the efforts of the Commission alone. It will need people to stop externalizing the problem and its solution. We can no longer wait for the 'messiah' to come and redeem us from this mess and need to find solutions within the framework of existing laws and structures, which we have enough of in place. All we need are people with the courage, willingness and the conviction to implement them. We need to begin by infusing a sense of pride in being a democracy. Creating a stake in good governance that benefits common citizens at large can no longer be a fad but is an essential pre-requisite for progress. The outrage and frustrations will have to be converted to active engagement with the system, and people will certainly find answers to the questions they have. The change begins with I, the citizen.

Making the right choice

The announcement of any election naturally creates an air of expectation. For the ordinary citizens, it is an opportunity to make a statement either in favor of or against the incumbent. For the politically ambitious, it is an opportunity to ascend their career ladders. For the political parties it is a time to make their calculations and look for the most winnable candidate within their ranks, or even outside. And for a whole lot of people, elections are a way of making a quick buck by running an assortment of errands for a party or a candidate ranging from organizing campaigns and rallies or mobilizing people to merely being present at a time and a place for show of numbers.

While parties get busy making their strategies, mobilizing resources and planning their events in addition to picking their candidates, we as citizens still have to face the question of who among the candidates is best suited to represent us. There may be limited choices, but it is a difficult proposition to answer the question, "How do I decide who to vote for?" Each candidate would have made his or her promise. Some would be driven by their manifestos and some by pure electoral mathematics. Some would play the card of caste or religion and some would promise the moon and some may even intimidate. We must remember that we ultimately will get the parliamentarians we deserve. Which means that we must be sure that the candidate is someone who can be trusted, is knowledgeable and will do the right thing for the constituency.

"But everyone is a thief!" "Nobody is above corruption!" "Nothing is going to change regardless of who I vote for!" These are common refrains during any conversation on who the best candidate is. A more nuanced dilemma is "I like the candidate, but not the party s/he belongs to" or "I just have to choose between the lesser of two or more evils". All these expressions are commonplace and yet, as a team of campaigners working towards ensuring corruption-free elections, we had to find suitable, convincing and positive responses to people's questions on who is the right candidate, and it was quite a challenge. We also had to keep our own political biases or preferences at an arm's length while responding.

While it would be very difficult to prove whether or not a person would remain honest or turn out to be a capable administrator even before electing him or her, we can still assess whether the person we are voting for deserves our vote or not. The first step in this direction indeed is to value our vote highly. And then find out whether the candidate is worthy enough of our vote by asking a few questions. Many of us tend to forget in the din of elections that, when contestants who are otherwise out-screaming each other, come to our doorstep, it is our prerogative to speak and to ask questions. As part of the campaign, we had prepared a range of questions for people to ask the candidates who approached them. They included questions about the basic background of the candidates to their stance on local, national and international issues, questions to gauge their knowledge on the day-to-day concerns of the constituency and their ideas on how they thought changes can be brought about. The list also had questions like how long they had been in politics and whether they had filed their Income Tax returns. We asked people to question the candidates' performance as a Member of Parliament if they had been one in the past or were currently holding that position, in terms of attendance in the Parliament, questions asked during sessions, and about utilization of development funds that are at their disposal. The candidates' familiarity with their own party manifestos to their positions on issues such as Universal Health Coverage or Food Security, their knowledge of the 73rd and 74th Constitutional Amendments and their ideas about tackling violence against women or of even keeping their offices accessible to the general public was also sought through these questions.

We had an interesting experience when we first took these questions to the people. They demanded the right answers to every question on the list. Our team was in a quandary as we did not want to bias people with what we may have felt as the right answers. A few people asked us how they could question if they didn't know the answers, but were convinced once the spirit behind the exercise was elucidated.

The point to be noted here is that one need not be an expert to ask these questions, nor does the contesting candidate need to be an expert on ALL matters, but the attitude and outlook of the candidates are necessarily on display even when a small list of simple questions is asked and their responses sought. The simplicity or the lack of, in their replies could give enough of a clue whether the candidates deserve a vote or not. More importantly, we discovered that equipping people with these questions can tend to have an empowering effect on them. Members of our team started exuding confidence when faced with challenging situations. Some people including media personnel even asked why these questions were not given to them earlier.

The lesson from this experience is simple, yet powerful. Making the right choice of candidates to represent us begins with asking the right questions. Somehow, over a period of time, elections have become more about contestants and parties and less about people. We as citizens have to claim our rightful space of prominence when it comes to elections and go beyond being mute spectators and anonymous voters. We are now equipped with an option of

NOTA[33] (None of the above) to express our dissatisfaction with all the candidates who have contested. It may be a step in the right direction, but definitely not enough to throw right candidates in the fray or for us to make a right choice based on a candidates' knowledge of issues and their approach to address them. If, in every Gram Panchayat election, City Municipal Corporation election, Legislative Assembly or Parliamentary election, we make the habit of asking questions, we may sooner rather than later be spoiled for choice. Making the right choice then may still be difficult, but it would be a happy problem to have.

33 NOTA or None of the above is an option provided by the Election Commission of India to Indian voters through a 2013 Supreme Court ruling that voters can use to indicate their disapproval with all candidates and prevent bogus voting. In the general elections of 2014, about 1.1% (6 million) of the voters opted NOTA.

Shoring up the decaying political discourse

As the dates for the Lok Sabha polls in 2014 got nearer, the decibel levels of the ongoing political discourse were getting shriller, but with issues of very little national significance. None of the parties or the key individual players seemed to be drawing the attention of the electorate to matters of collective national good. The little noise that one person or party was making regarding corruption, crony capitalism and dynastic politics got drowned in the party's own theatrics and television antics. While one expected political rallies and public speeches to provide opportunities to communicate the key messages reflecting the socio-economic concerns, political ideologies and the parties' thoughts and opinions on policy matters, all that they were reduced to was demonstrating their numerical strength, visibility in media and financial clout.

Indian democracy is known to be noisy and unhealthy. Parliamentary elections provide the ideal platform for issues of national significance to be brought to the center-stage and foster discussion on the general direction that the nation is likely to move towards. However political debates had reached a nadir in the run-up to the 2014 elections and whether it was in media or in public meetings, most parties resorted to berating the other rather than engage in constructive dialogue. The quality of political discourse does indicate the health of the democracy and hence one of the ways of making our democracy healthier is to enhance the quality of debate and discourse during elections.

While emotions and other factors rather than mere reason are known to guide the voter in choosing his or her representative, one also needs to appreciate that s/he cannot be taken for granted and fed with morning headlines that are bereft of any serious content. Most of the discussions during the elections revolved around ghost issues created ostensibly to divert people's thoughts and concerns from the real and burning problems on hand. One leader calling another a Pakistani terrorist and another one wanting to chop his rival party's leader to pieces dominated headlines for a couple of days. Insensitive remarks about gender, a senior political leader asking his constituents to vote twice (illegally), statements that could stir up religious divides and challenges to the Election Commission itself were the order of the day.

With a media only happy to feed off sensationalism, all that this resulted in was taking the focus away from how the nation needs to brace itself in dealing with the growing menace of terror-related violence, the problem of Naxalism[34] and its deeper realities, or issues related to hunger, malnutrition, education or healthcare. Neither internal security matters nor issues related to gender violence seem to attract any clarity of thought beyond being treated as 'vote catching' slogans. There was hardly any debate on the energy crisis facing India or on how to redefine our nuclear policy, keeping both the changing international perception towards nuclear power, the local needs of the country and the extremely vital aspects of transparency and safety standards. The concern about the issues of environmental pollution and social justice against the backdrop of the desire to rapidly industrialize and join the global bandwagon of mindless consumerism was barely raised.

These and several other issues affect millions of people and except for few individuals and civil society groups, neither the

34 Naxalism is a form of far-left and radical ideology that aligns with Maoist political sentiments. The term came into being after a village named Naxalbari in the state of West Bengal, where a peasant uprising took place in 1967, but was eventually quelled by the state.

media, nor the political class seemed interested in raising them. It is surprising and scary how people's real issues do not figure in the campaigns where their votes are needed. Despite the formation of many committees, the nation is yet to have a scientifically validated poverty assessment process. We are still arguing about the different percentages of people below the poverty line in India, clearly derailing our understanding of poverty, the metrics of poverty and the processes to alleviate poverty. It is indeed sad that not a single party made this an issue of electoral significance. There was hardly any political or media space debating the impending danger of 'policy capture' by the elite, the rich and powerful and corporate India. Electoral funding by large corporate houses has the danger of being seen as investments, the returns of which will be amenable policies that will come later.

In one constituency, there was a debate on *Aadhaar*, the initiative to provide a Unique Identification Number to resident Indian citizens, but it was reduced to 'noise', with the real and deeper issues of spending huge sums of money on a scheme/program that had no legislative sanction being completely brushed aside. Issues of data privacy and abuse of the information stored did not seem to find much space in the ongoing debate. Neither did rational and long-term geopolitical policy involving our relations with the neighboring countries including China and Pakistan, other than the usual rhetoric. Despite being unsure about how to manage the changing comfort levels with USA or how to deal with our long-time ally Russia, one could gather from the debates that foreign policy was a foreign topic in the din of electoral promises.

Economic concerns including stimulating the primary land-based economy and creating an environment to promote the growth of the manufacturing sector did not seem to flow from an understanding of the ground realities and the evidence that stares us on the face. There was no debate by any party on how they view the youth of the country and how they intend to capitalize on the 'demographic dividend'. Debates seemed to harbor around merely giving tickets to younger people, while the larger issues of engaging meaningfully with the youth, creating opportunities for them or facilitating skill development to participate in the mainstream economy took a backseat.

Except occasional articles by concerned activists and intellectuals, there was little discourse on Universal Health Access, rational drug policy (including the use of generic drugs), the burgeoning problem of adulterated and poor quality drugs, and the growing burden of non-communicable diseases and on how to deal with them. No clarity was apparent in any party's thinking on how they intended to improve the learning outcomes of the millions of children in our primary schools despite spending millions of rupees for more than a decade now. Improving higher education seemed to be limited to increasing the number of universities without looking at the funda-mental reforms that the sector is crying for. The electorate could not know whether any major party was even considering increasing the allocation to health and education sectors in %GDP terms.

Corruption did figure in the election debates, but there was little information provided by the political parties on how they intended to stem the growth of 'collusive corruption' that has been the bane of not just the public sector but also the private and NGO sectors. The political debate seemed to focus more on stronger laws without a fundamental understanding of the fact that Indian society has to now move towards not merely 'fighting corruption' but 'fighting to stay honest'.

Issues of good governance, metrics for measuring the work of government and public servants, citizen centric polices including social accountability processes and creating opportunities for lateral entry of competent and deserving people into higher levels of the bureaucracy should necessarily constitute contemporary political debates, but the parties either did not have the will or the capa-bility to raise them and let their stances be known. Similarly, issues such as management of fiscal policies and subsidies, Center-State relations and strengthening federal structures and democratic institutions were topics that very few parties seemed to be ready to bring up. It would have required a deeper understanding of the issues in operationalizing the 73rd and 74th Constitutional amendments and how decentralization could go beyond just transfer of funds and functions to our Urban Local Bodies and Gram Panchayats. The election frenzy, it seemed, did not allow such a space.

The plethora of aforementioned issues are the ones that really affect people. Yet, how is it that political parties get away without touching upon them, election after election? How is it that parties and their candidates are able to whip up debates and grab media attention on frivolous issues even as the nation is faced with critical development concerns? The only answer is that there is not enough pressure on the political class created by the electorate. If citizens can take control of the debate and start setting the agenda, the political class as well as media would be forced to respond. It would have to begin with reasoned and informed debates in local circles with elected representatives or aspirants, who would then have to convey the prevailing mood of the electorate to the decision makers within their parties.

The citizenry needs to begin by asking the key questions to parties and their candidates. Unless we set the pace, intensity and quality of the debate, politicians will only dish out colorful but empty issues that reflect the society that they represent. The media has to take the lead in bringing these issues to the surface and go beyond mere opinion polls and debating electoral arithmetic.

Political debates and public discourse on politics of the nation are the lifeblood of democracy. With Indians known to be articulate and argumentative, all that is needed is a shift towards real issues from the sensational, superficial topics. Together, we need to communicate to our political system that the time has come for them, and us to shore up the decaying political discourse in a bid to improve and maintain the health of our democracy.

The role of the manifesto

A manifesto is a public declaration of intent, motives and positions of an individual or a group in general, and in the context of elections that of an independent candidate or a political party. It is also a promise to the people at large, on the basis of which an individual or a political party seeks power to represent those people. Though it may serve to reflect the ideology of the political unit, a manifesto may be deemed apropos only if it reflects the real will and aspirations of people, aligns with the spirit of the Constitution and remains relevant even after the elections are over. Whether political parties – national, regional or local – comprehend this spirit and stay true to it is anybody's guess. If we analyze the level and content of political discourse preceding any of the elections held in India in the last decade, or look at the promises that candidates make to their constituency, one may feel that the manifesto has just become a token document and is hardly given the importance it deserves.

Yet, there are civil society initiatives before elections to draft people's manifestos based on the real needs and issues of people and to present it to political parties for consideration. It is before the elections that contesting candidates and parties are most willing to listen to people and it is an opportune moment for people to state their concerns. As part of the 'Making Democracy Work' campaign, we took upon ourselves the task of reaching out to the political parties and highlighting issues and points that they needed to include in their manifestos. Before the Legislative Assembly elections of Karnataka in 2013, we consulted the likes of Former Chief Justice of India M N Venkatachaliah and sent letters signed by him to the offices of all major political parties in Karnataka at that time.

These letters demanded that the parties commit to a development agenda based on certain democratic principles. One top priority was pursuing decentralization and supporting citizen engagement through the implementation of the 73rd and 74th amendments to the Constitution of India in letter and spirit. Demands for transparency and accountability, citizen friendly budgets, commitment to food security through universalization of public distribution system, implementing the Right to Education and universal access to healthcare were other crucial points that found mention in the letter. Commitment to protection of environment and sustainability along with measures to protect the interests of marginalized populations such as forest based tribal communities, were highlighted. Importantly, the document asked the political parties to show commitment towards strengthening democracy by engaging in fair electoral practices by not engaging in any kind of influencing of voters by way of kind, cash, favors or threats to citizens; ensuring democratic practices within the functioning of their party; paving the way for adequate representation of women and people from marginalized sections in the list of contesting candidates; and restricting candidates with criminal backgrounds from contesting the elections.

These points were not necessarily new themes or ideas for new programs, but already envisioned and provided for by the Constitution of India. The fact that we had to reiterate them and ask political parties to include them in their manifestos is an indicator of how far removed we are from the spirit of our Constitution when it comes to electoral promises and expectations. The preamble to the Constitution of India, in fact served as the source of our inspiration and values.

Our efforts to influence the manifestos did not cease with the dispatch of the letters. The contents of Justice Venkatachaliah's letter to political parties were published by local print media in the form of a citizen's request. I was also invited to be on an advisory panel by another widely read daily to draft a People's Manifesto, which appeared as a special feature. However, it was difficult for us to set any expectations from this exercise. To our pleasant surprise, we got positive responses from both regional and national political parties. While the president of the manifesto committee of a national party personally visited GRAAM for a discussion on the subject, we found that the points mentioned in our draft had found space in the manifesto released by at least two other parties, especially those on food security and public health. The response was encouraging enough for us to consider continuing our advocacy efforts on election manifestos in the following year when the Parliamentary elections were held in India.

What remains a challenge though, is to get large numbers of people to engage in dialogue with the political class on manifestos. Most political parties know that they can get away with promising paltry freebies, while the manifestos are reflective of the larger intent and programs which one may assume that the party would launch, if voted to power. The question we have to ask ourselves is whether we, as citizens are ready to vote based on manifestos. Are we ready to shed caste and kinship, forgo short-term gains or ignore biases such as personas or figureheads and vote for those who have voiced concerns on our issues in their manifestos? Can we as citizens make the manifestos our starting point for engagement with the political class, especially during elections? Can we demand that promises made by parties and candidates be articulated in their manifestos and hold them accountable to the commitments made?

There is also a debate on whether the manifestos should be made legally binding on the parties. This would ensure that the manifestos don't become a token document during elections and something that is drafted for the sake of formality. The trend in fact is worrying. During the general elections held in 2014, major national parties had delayed releasing their manifestos almost until only a week was left before the nation went to polls. In a recent state election, one major national party declared that it did not have a manifesto and only a set of guiding principles. Both these approaches are problematic and against the spirit of democracy, as they only serve to keep the electorate in the dark. And so is the fact that manifestos or their contents are rendered irrelevant once the parties are in power. In the event of a post-election coalition of parties staking claim to form the government, it is political conveniences and power equations that rule the roost. But we've also seen governments formed by parties with clear majorities in the House go back on the promises made in their manifestos.

Legally binding or not, the time has surely come for citizens to take action and make election manifestos relevant. Firstly, in terms of content, it should reflect people's issues and concerns; secondly it should be a basis on which they would cast their votes; and thirdly it should be a tool to hold political parties accountable to the promises they've made to the people. Evolution and enhancement of the role of manifestos is a crucial aspect of a slew of electoral reforms that our country needs. This can be brought about by an enlightened citizenry with minimal assistance either from the executive or the judiciary. And, on the day when a party can claim to have won an election on the basis of its manifesto and its endorsement by the people, we can safely say that electoral politics as well as the Indian electorate has matured to a new level.

"EVEN WHEN LAWS HAVE BEEN
WRITTEN DOWN, THEY OUGHT NOT
ALWAYS TO REMAIN UNALTERED."

ARISTOTLE

Perspectives on policy

Policy decisions of a state are macro decisions made on the basis of aggregated information, but are of consequence to millions of people who live far away from the nerve-centers of policy making. It is therefore appropriate that we appreciate the view from the ground in addition to the aspects that the state's policy makers in high positions take into consideration. In these times when policy capture by the elite and the powerful is disconcertingly real, development interventionists as well as policy advocates would do well to be mindful of this fact and counter it with evidence-based, on-the-ground realities. The voice and perspectives of the people for whom the policies matter *must* find greater space in the entire policy discourse.

This section comprises my perspectives on public policies in a few themes that are critical to human development. These are perspectives that have evolved over a period of time based on my engagement with people at the grassroots and an understanding of policy making and its principles through experience and education. Though it may not always be explicitly articulated, the articles attempt to echo a belief in incorporating grassroots perspectives and people's participation in policy making, its implementation and feedback on a continuous basis so that the policies are rendered sound and relevant.

Valuing life

Bomma, a Jenukuruba, lived in Vodeyarahallimala tribal colony on the fringes of Bandipur forest in Mysuru district with his wife and three little children. He did not have a regular income and his worry each day was about finding some employment locally in order to keep the hearth in his little hut burning. His wife Chinnamma took care of the children, but was additionally burdened with his drinking habits and the entire family survived with nothing more than a hand to mouth existence. Being landless, they depended on the nearby forests for their sustenance.

It was a Tuesday and seemed like any other day. Chinnamma saw her husband off at their hut and asked him to return early with firewood for her cooking. It was a routine exercise to fetch firewood from the 'restricted' forests, which was once their home. Bomma was accompanied by another tribal into the forest and Chinnamma set about her own chores. A couple of hours had passed by when she rushed out of her hut after hearing a lot of commotion in the hamlet. People were running around helpless and confused. It was after a neighbor explained to her about what had happened, that reality started sinking into her. As Bomma and his friend walked towards the forest, an elephant attacked them. Bomma fell as he was running and was trampled to death. His friend had come running back and had broken the news. The men folk were now grouping together to go and bring the body back. When she saw her husband off, little had she realized that she would never see him alive again. In all this commotion, her world had come to a still and her sense of security gone.

What or who killed Bomma is a recurring question to me even today. Did the elephant only terminate a process of dying that began sometime in the mid-seventies? For generations, Bomma and his people had lived in the forests with no worry about yesterday or concern for tomorrow. Bomma's ancestors never really knew hunger or poverty. The forests gave them all that they needed. Their food comprised the roots, berries, honey and meat from the deer or wild boar that they would occasionally hunt. The year 1972 changed all that. The Government of India brought in the Forest Conservation Act and the forests that Bomma's people loved and cherished were declared as National Parks. His people were told that they were foreigners in their own land and all rights that they enjoyed vis-à-vis the forests were extinguished. They were evicted from the forests and forcibly settled in inhuman habitations on its fringes. They were suddenly exposed to mainstream society and were in a situation where they could neither integrate into a society and its norms they understood little about nor could they go back to the comfort zones of their forests. They lacked the skills to acculturate and their only skill of collecting honey was of little economic value outside the forests. The whole process had condemned Bomma and his people to a world they could never fully comprehend.

The local Range Forest Officer at the time of Bomma's death was a young man yet to be hardened by the system. He was humane and sensitive to the situation and put his best efforts to ensure that his recommendation to the government for compensation would be filed and accepted. However, determining a fit compensation is something more than arriving at a sum of money. Especially for those people who have hardly traded with money or ever valued their assets – their forests, their birds, their trees, roots and berries, the lifestyle bestowed upon them by a natural world – in monetary terms. A monetary compensation of a hundred and fifty thousand rupees was eventually given to Chinnamma to continue to live bereft of the little security she had.

Not only is our system incapable of determining the value of one's life, it is also grossly unfair when it attempts to do so. The compensation that Chinnamma received begets the question of how the government determined that Bomma's life was worth only that much, whereas a railway accident victim would have received more and an air-crash victim's family would have received several times more money in the form of compensation. How does one determine the fair value of a human life? How can one say that the life of a politician, a bureaucrat or a modern-day professional is more valuable than that of a farmer or a rural artisan? Or, for that matter, how are the lives of people who are victims of displacement, industrial disasters or calamities in countries like India valued in comparison with those in the first world?

This is not to say that financial compensation is not useful or necessary. I am also conscious that money alone cannot restore everything that accompanies loss of lives. What we need is a more sensitive approach in determining the value of compensation that goes beyond economic and political considerations. The final amount of compensation and the manner in which it is disbursed must take multiple factors into consideration and try to positively impact the lives of the kin of the deceased. It must take into account not just the socio-economic background of the person, but the accountability of agencies that might have led to death or injury of people.

Is the government justified in looking at Bomma's death and the immediate incidents leading to it in isolation? What about the government's inability to comprehend how inseparable indigenous communities are from their forests? How can we compensate the failure of a system that is unable to grasp why even decades after being forced out of forests, these communities are yet to be equipped with skills to cope with the demands of mainstream life and society? Would better implementation of the government's various development schemes including the Forest Rights Act, 2006[35] have prevented the death of Bomma or provided him and his family a higher social and economic status?

It is also of concern that in the entire episode, one hardly finds the voice of the people at its center heard. At no stage were Bomma's people in a position to determine anything for themselves. Wouldn't true democracy be about finding space for their expression of what their lives, livelihoods and aspirations are all about, in the midst of laws and programs? An attempt was made by the Forest Rights Act, 2006 that gave the traditionally forest dwelling and forest dependent communities some power and say in the decisions about their forests and other resources. Though these structures are democratic in some sense, they are still new to many indigenous communities and it would take years, if not decades for the people to evolve and make them meaningful. But, persist we must. Recent developments indicate that there are likely to be dilutions in the act ostensibly to ease investment and promote 'development'. A failure to listen to the voice of the people from the grassroots would lead to the slow deaths of many a Bomma and his people. And, others would calculate the value of the lives faded out and feel that the money given will be compensation enough.

---

35 The Scheduled Tribes and Other Traditional Forest Dwellers (Recognition of Forest Rights) Act, 2006 was passed by the Indian Parliament in December 2006 accords rights of access to land and resources of the forest to forest-dwelling individuals and communities, which they had otherwise been denied for decades.

Malnutrition – a national shame

In 2012, a report was released by the then Prime Minister Manmohan Singh on the state of childhood malnutrition in India, which prompted him to declare malnutrition as a 'national shame'. The report mentioned that 42 percent of children in India below five years are malnourished. There are reports from other credible agencies as well that put the figure closer to between 52 and 54 percent. The statistic itself may astound or baffle someone in the world of academics, policy or development economics, but what does it mean to an average Indian?

As I mull over these figures, I recollect my experiences in Sahebganj district of Jharkhand more than a decade ago, especially my visits to a couple of families belonging to the Mal Paharia tribe. While a little rice and a watery gravy to accompany it, formed the main meal of one family which had five children, in another house I found a family of seven – three adults and four children – hovering around an aluminum plate filled with four thick *rotis*[36] and a few slices of onion and three long chillies that were lying on the ground beside the plate. This was lunch for the entire family and their largest meal of the day too. If this is an everyday reality for millions of families across India, it would not be a surprise if we are called a nation of the malnourished.

The statistics related to malnutrition in India present a very grim picture. As per UNICEF, malnutrition is more common in

36 Indian bread usually made of wheat flour

India than sub-Saharan Africa with a third of all malnourished children living in India and half of all childhood deaths being linked to malnutrition. Statistics reveal that around 46 percent of all Indian children below the age of three are too small for their age, 47 percent of them are underweight and at least 16 percent are wasted[37]. It is further estimated that one third of all women are underweight ostensibly due to various social and economic factors that affect their growth right from childhood. Inadequate care of women and girls, especially during pregnancy further results in low birth-weight babies. Nearly 30 percent of all new-borns have a low birth-weight, making them vulnerable to further malnutrition and disease.

Yet, these statistics mean little to the Mal Paharia family in Sahebganj and millions of other such families. Malnourishment is the result of not just lack of food and nutrition, but also poor access to health services, hygiene practices, quality of care that the woman has received in her pregnancy and post-delivery and other social determinants. Even more concerning is the fact that malnourishment, especially in the early years of the child can result in adverse long-term consequences and almost invariably affects girls more than boys. UNICEF further asserts that malnutrition in early childhood has serious, long-term consequences because it impedes motor, sensory, cognitive, social and emotional development. Malnourished children are less likely to perform well in school and more likely to grow into malnourished adults, are at greater risk of disease and early death.

A paper published by the World Bank's Human Development Network rightly notes that as a result of the commonly held perception that food insecurity is the primary or even sole cause of malnutrition, the existing response to malnutrition in India has been skewed towards food-based interventions and has placed little emphasis on schemes addressing the other determinants of

---

37 Wasting or acute malnutrition is a condition accompanied by rapid loss of weight or failure to gain weight and can be linked to mortality

malnutrition. In addition to targeting children below three years of age, any program related to the issue must also focus on nutrition and health education, care and behavioral aspects, hygiene and safe drinking water, and importantly people's participation. Needless to add, it must be accompanied by the strengthening of the primary health care delivery system.

The global community had designated halving the prevalence of underweight children by 2015 as a key indicator of progress towards the Millennium Development Goal (MDG) of eradicating extreme poverty and hunger. These targets mean little to the poor and vulnerable families of India, which has been on a development model based on economic growth for almost a quarter of a century now. Economic growth alone, however impressive, will not help meet the nutrition targets. In fact, that would be a flawed argument as it is only by effectively combating under-nutrition, that India will reap benefits in terms of human development and economic returns. When there are approximately sixty million under-weight children in India, whose health, education and productivity are impacted, one can easily conclude that persistent under-nutrition is an impediment to economic growth. However, there is little evidence to suggest that this has been comprehended by the proponents of market economy and neo-liberal policies that are driving India today.

It is not that the government in India has not responded to the situation. A slew of measures to address the issue of food security have been undertaken with programs and schemes on the ground such as mid-day meals for all children in government schools and various nutrition programs under the Integrated Child Development Scheme (ICDS). The Government of India has even brought in a legislation, the National Food Security Act 2013, which makes access to various food security programs a legal entitlement of citizens. Though some ground has been covered through ICDS and its supplementary feeding programs, there is little that has been addressed for children below three years of age, the very age range in which serious problems related to malnutrition could set in.

It is a matter of serious concern that the present government has cut the budget allocations to ICDS, the key program towards ensuring food and nutrition security of young children. It is hard to fathom the rationale behind the cut especially when plans were afoot to intensify the efforts to tackle the problem of malnutrition in women and children under the National Nutrition Mission, not so long ago. The fund cuts would also delay any substantial increase in the honorarium paid to Anganwadi[38] workers, who are the backbone of implementing programs related to nutrition on the ground.

What is needed today instead is a reform and strengthening of the existing nutrition programs that take into account traditional food patterns of communities, issues of food safety, hygiene, access to clean drinking water on the one hand and awareness building and participation of communities on the other. The concern over budget cuts and the fact that it will affect 300 million poor families has been raised by the government's own Ministry of Women and Child Development, but its voice needs to be backed by the citizenry and the representatives of the affected communities. As citizens who aspire that India should be a leading nation in the world on multiple fronts, we need to remember that we cannot be deemed a developed nation as long as there are families like the ones in Sahebganj, whose aspirations do not go beyond securing the next meal. It is for all of us to steer the focus of the government towards ensuring that we wipe this national shame off India's record.

---

38 Anganwadis are government run centers located in all villages established with the aim of addressing the issue of malnutrition, especially among children. They are part of the Women and Child Welfare system which provide supplementary nutrition, non-formal pre-school education, nutrition and health education, counseling as well as immunization, health check-up and referral services.

FDI in retail – a death knell for Rathnamma

Every morning Rathnamma sat on the footpath[39] outside my house in Mysuru selling greens and vegetables. She came at around eight am on most days and went about her business that lasted not more than two to three hours. Her everyday enterprise had drawn my attention and I was curious to know more about the transactions of her business; how much she could possibly earn each day and how she made her ends meet. One day I decided to talk to her and understand all that I wanted.

From our conversation, I learned that Rathnamma would borrow 500 rupees every day from a money lender to buy the greens and vegetables each morning directly from farmers from an 'unofficial' market, not far from the grand palace in the heart of Mysuru. She would then spend about fifty rupees transporting the vegetables to this spot of hers in an auto-rickshaw. Her clientele naturally included residents of my neighborhood who were indeed fortunate to be able to buy from her, vegetables that were possibly as fresh as one could get in the city. By the time she wrapped up her business for the day, she earned around 750 rupees. She would have to return 550 rupees to the money lender in the evening and the 150 rupees or so left added to her family's income.

I was fascinated by her story and the economics associated

39 A sidewalk that may or may not be paved

with it. Her family, the money lender, the farmers involved and the auto driver were all involved directly in this economy besides many others who were directly or indirectly impacted. Besides, this cycle continued day after day, bringing a certain predictability and vulnerability at the same time.

The conversation with Rathnamma helped me appreciate the simple but fragile everyday economics that sustained her and millions of families like hers'. As we conversed, I tried to put the controversy that India witnessed in early 2012 over allowing Foreign Direct Investment (FDI) in the retail sector into context. There was so much heat and little light in the discussions that took place in the Parliament of India before the government of the day decided to put the decision on hold. There were arguments for and against FDI in retail in the Parliament, in classrooms, over the internet and on television shows. My venture was to see the issue from 'ground zero', from where people like Rathnamma lived and transacted their business.

Before we draw our conclusions, we need to understand what retail business is, why foreign players are interested in doing this business in India and what the experiences of other countries like China, Indonesia and Vietnam have been. Would our country and the economy benefit from FDI in retail? How are the average small traders and Indian farmers going to be protected? While the country's aggregate economy grows, will FDI in retail swallow up the poor in the process? There are several questions to deliberate upon.

Retail is that space and interface where a product is traded so that it reaches its final intended user or consumer. The Delhi High Court, in fact, defined the term 'retail' as a sale for final consumption in contrast to a sale for further sale or processing. For a nation with 1.25 billion people, the retail sector is undeniably a buzzing sector with tremendous potential for growth and for people to contribute to it as well as be benefited from it.

In India, this sector is dominated by unorganized retail

comprising owner-manned general stores, the local *kirana* (provision) stores, petty corner shops, push-cart and pavement vendors among others. It is estimated that India is among the countries with the highest number of retail outlets per inhabitant in the world. These traditional formats, apart from having numerous participants in the value chain have a certain ethos and socio-cultural dynamics about them including a sense of community. Unorganized retail in India is also fragmented in nature and typically suffers from limited access to capital, labor and real-estate options. The typical traditional retailer follows the low-cost-and-size format, functioning at a small-scale level, rarely liable for tax and has a low-cost operating model. It is also claimed that the explosion of retail and the high number of retail outlets per inhabitant reflects disguised employment and is indicative of a lack of suitable employment opportunities for people.

On the other hand organized retail comprises essentially licensed traders, merchants and companies and their most visible presence includes the corporate backed supermarkets, hypermarkets and retail chains. In India, large business conglomerates such as Tata group, Reliance, Birla and Bharti have entered the organized retail space while others such as RPG, Spencers Retail, Future Group and Lifestyle Retail have retail as the key segments of their business.

Overall, the retail sector makes a contribution of about 14% to India's GDP and employs 7% of its workforce, making it the largest source of employment, second only to agriculture. It is estimated that unorganized retail accounts for more than 95% of the total trade in the sector and employs close to 40 million people, whereas the workforce strength of organized retail stands at five hundred thousand. Estimates vary widely about the true size of the retail business in India. Some have estimated that it is around 135 billion dollars and that it is growing at a rate of 40% per annum, while others estimate it to be worth 500 billion dollars or more. Undoubtedly, this sector is a key pillar of the Indian economy and with the rise in disposable incomes among the burgeoning middle-class and increased consumerism, is poised to be a critical part of India's 'growth' story.

Against this backdrop, the clamor for opening up the sector for Foreign Direct Investment has also increased in the country, especially in the last decade. Despite being a highly emotive and politically sensitive issue, successive governments have so far treaded gradually in the direction of allowing increased foreign participation in the retail sector, while being conscious of and letting political compulsions dictate the pace of retail sector reforms.

The process started in 1997 with 100% FDI being allowed in cash and carry wholesale, albeit with government approval, and this continued until 2006 when terms were relaxed. Along with it, up to 51% investment in single-brand retail outlets was also permitted. In January 2012, this cap was removed, but conditions were attached to it, which included sourcing of at least 30% of the value of products from small Indian industries, cottage industries, local artisans, craftsmen, etc. Big brands such as furniture major IKEA have found this restrictive and announced postponement of their plans in India despite showing early enthusiasm. The next major step taken in retail sector reforms was that of allowing up to 51% foreign direct investment in multi-brand retail, throwing open doors to major players like Walmart, Carrefour, Tesco and others. This has, by far been the most hotly debated aspect in the entire discourse on FDI in retail.

One of the key arguments in favor of allowing FDI in retail is that it stands to boost the economy by generating jobs, encouraging investment in infrastructure and resulting in higher tax revenues. Other than that, efficient supply chain infrastructure including better warehousing, cold-storage and cold-chains, increased consumer choice and improved experience are touted as advantages. The government for its part contends that by allowing large multi-nationals to set up multi-brand retail outlets in Indian towns with populations of more than one million, there is scope for big ticket players and smaller stores to coexist and flourish. Such cities would absorb and support the large stores, while also allowing other players including niche traders to carry out their businesses. The move would help the process of training a large number of youth across the country to work and grow in formal workplaces, access the benefits of organized employment and make them upwardly mobile. The place and role of FDI in retail in the emergence of India as an economic superpower, it may seem, has been scripted to perfection.

In reality, the scenario is much more complex. When big players like Walmart set up their retail operations, they create superstores that would sell typically everything – from vegetables to the latest electronic gadgets – at extremely low prices that will most likely undercut those in nearby stores selling similar goods. With deep pockets to absorb the 'losses', these players can easily outlive the other traditional traders through predatory pricing and by reorienting the established supply chain of goods. While it is argued that reduction of intermediaries or middle-men, who are often touted as villains, would result in passing the price benefits to consumers, one must not ignore the pressure that these players are able to exert on the supply side by forcing preordained quantities and specifications of products at lower cost prices. Especially in the food production sector, mono-cropping and exploitative contract farming are attributed to the pressures of supplying to Walmart and their ilk who create a monopoly situation with few escape routes for small producers and farmers. Thus, there is every possibility that increased flow and thereby control of foreign capital in the retail sector will lead into a situation that has enormous social and economic ramifications, but one that may be out of control.

Examples of China, Malaysia and Thailand are often quoted to support FDI in retail not just because the sector employs a large workforce and contributes significantly to the GDP of the respective countries, but also because of the local opposition to foreign investment in retail that these countries had initially seen, just like in India. But one must also not forget the fact that these countries, who opened their retail sector to FDI in the recent past, have been forced to enact new laws to check the prolific expansion of the new foreign malls and hypermarkets. With a poor record of India's politicians and bureaucrats in ensuring that regulatory laws are followed and frameworks are adhered to, the experiences of these countries may not be good benchmarks for us. Whether foreign investment by way of FDI translates into foreign exchange reserves of the country or in the form of assets and the issue of repatriation of profits are different debates altogether.

Yet again, we find that the voice of those who are likely to be most affected by a policy decision are hardly taken into account. While there are arguments about the advantages and pitfalls of allowing FDI in retail, we must try and look at this issue from the eyes of Rathnamma and traders like her. Her small pavement shop may not seem to be adding to the growing economy, but it ensures food on her table. Will the producers and traders at the lowest level like her be able to cope with the dynamics of a reformed retail sector and find themselves a place to sustain and grow? Will someone like Rathnamma, after being uprooted from her traditional form of business, be able to compete with young English-speaking helpers who would be in demand? Or for that matter find other areas of work and acquire new skills to sustain herself?

What the governments at the center and in the states need to do is go beyond advocating the cause of these large corporations and start creating an enabling environment that will allow her access to more reasonable credit and a formal market system. Addressing the insecurities and risks that millions of people like Rathnamma face and protecting them should be the first priority of the government rather than protecting the interests of big ticket investors. The prevailing skew in priorities is a threat to democratic decision making and it is vital that this skew is addressed. Only then can we, as citizens feel more reassured that policy decisions such as allowing FDI in retail have been taken in the interest of the nation at large, rather than by keeping in consideration the benefits of only a selected few.

Fighting poverty through the Right to Education Act

A few years back, I was traveling through the villages of Nanjangud Taluk of Mysuru district. I met a man named Kempaiah, who was close to sixty years at that time. He sounded depressed and alone, and was coughing continuously. I learned that it had been a few weeks since his wife and children had temporarily moved to the neighboring district of Kodagu, and were employed in a coffee estate there. This was inevitable, he reckoned, as they could each earn nearly five hundred rupees every day over there. That was an amount he could only dream about earning in his own village where the maximum wages that one could get was a hundred and fifty rupees for a day's labor. He could not even get this as most people refused to employ him, as they found him too feeble to do any kind of manual work. Staying alone with no employment and his immediate family not being around made him feel depressed and lost. All that he could now do was to wait for his son to come once a month and give him money for his sustenance.

Kempaiah had three children and the eldest one had dropped out of school in his ninth grade. This boy had been the most intelligent in his family and Kempaiah had hoped that he would be able to study further and at least get a college degree. But poverty had other plans. The boy had to drop out of school in order to take up a job and support his family. Three years down the line, he was the principal wage earner for the family and he could now only dream of the education that he could have had. Kempaiah was not only poor himself but had also managed to condemn his son to a life of poverty. Education could have meant an upward movement for his son, but that was not to be. Poverty alleviation programs such as the subsidized food grains under PDS and the rural employment guarantee scheme were at best getting the family to cope with poverty, but not getting them out of the poverty trap. Considering that 25% of the world's poor live in India on the one hand and the demographic dividend on the other, there is no time like now to address problem of inter-generational poverty through all means possible.

Around the same time, a few private schools in Bengaluru in Karnataka State had approached the courts asking for redressal from implementing some of the provisions of the Right to Education (RTE) Act. The RTE Act or the Right of Children to Free and Compulsory Education Act, introduced by the Parliament of India in 2009 and brought into effect from April 2010 onwards makes education a fundamental right of all children in India from the ages of six to fourteen. Among the notable provisions of this act is the requirement that all private educational institutions, except those run for minority communities, reserve 25% of the seats for poor children and children from other categories deemed as backward.

It was this provision that the private school managements were concerned about and were struggling with the idea of inter-mixing students from different social and economic classes. Off the record, they shared with me that this would be a challenge and that there was some resistance and reluctance about it. It is indeed shameful that they felt that the poor should not mix with the rich. While one can easily feel angered and agitated at this stance, we must realize it is perhaps a reflection of the society we live in and also appreciate the challenges that one will face in ensuring equity for all.

There are, without a doubt, challenges in implementation of the provisions of the act, but none that cannot be tackled. The state as well as the educational institutions have a role to play in it and must commit to the act's vision of providing quality education even to the children from the poorer sections of the society. Consider the fact that till recently, the annual income ceiling in Karnataka state for a family to seek admission for its child in a private school under the RTE was three hundred and fifty thousand rupees a year. With that kind of a ceiling even children of mid-career government employees were eligible to seek admissions under RTE quota in private schools. It remains unclear how the government arrived at the figure, but suffice it to say that continuing with the ceiling would be of no consequence to the real poor. In the rural areas, where majority of the schools are run by the government, most of the 'beneficiaries' are the ones who have money to buy fake income certificates. It is estimated that in Karnataka, nearly 94% of children in rural areas go to government schools. The High Court of Karnataka has since directed the government to revise the ceiling to a hundred thousand rupees in response to a petition challenging the government's norms. However, more needs to be done to ensure that the provisions of the act go to the deserving poor.

The state can simply introduce a slew of measures that includes tighter controls in issuing income certificates, preference for lowest of the lower income groups, making children of government employees who avail several other benefits ineligible and most importantly by putting in place a better and more pragmatic poverty assessment mechanism.

Ensuring that RTE is implemented in its true spirit also depends heavily on the stance that the private institutions take vis-à-vis discriminatory treatment between children who are admitted into the schools from their regular channels and those who have come through the reservation policy of the RTE Act. The schools must provide facilities like transport, food and other facilities like special classes or opportunities to participate in extra-curricular activities to all children at par. This is a gray area that is often cited by private institutions as a concern because they receive funding from the government in the form of reimbursements based on the per-child expenditure incurred by the state. And when the reimbursements from the government are delayed, the schools make 'losses'.

We must not forget that the government is bound constitutionally to provide its children with quality education. It cannot disown this responsibility and transfer it conveniently to the private sector. Let us not forget that the government is led by 'utilitarian' motives, while the private sector is led by 'profit' motives. The government cannot absolve itself from improving the quality of education in its own schools. It needs to ensure that good quality teachers are recruited, they are well-trained and oriented to teach in these rural schools and the entire system including the school administrators are held accountable for delivering quality education. It needs to bring on board the local communities and civil society organizations in doing this. Only when this happens can acts like the RTE go beyond mere education and help the country tackle the problems of poverty and inequity.

Very few people look at the Right to Education Act as a tool to fight intergenerational poverty. It is only when more children from socio-economically vulnerable backgrounds get the benefit of quality education at little or no cost that they would be able to extricate themselves out of the poverty trap and secure for themselves and their families a relatively poverty-free future. Quality education would mean avenues for higher education, better livelihoods and the growth of self-esteem. The Right to Education is not just an act ensuring education for all, but one that enshrines a spirit of ensuring equity and social justice for all. It is also easily one of the most significant social legislations passed by any country in recent times. It's a law that every Indian citizen should be proud of and be vigilant towards its abuse and misuse. Millions of children like Kempaiah's son have dreams in their eyes about climbing up the social and economic ladder. The RTE Act provides a unique scope for the state, its citizens and private institutions to work together and fructify those dreams.

Overcoming a poor understanding of poverty

It was sometime in 2010 that I met Ramaiah in Bengaluru. He lived with his wife, three children and elderly mother on the outskirts of the city. His life was very simple and revolved only around ensuring food on the table for his family. Every morning he would set out to the city and find work at one of the many construction sites. He was paid by the day and had no other form of security. His son was fifteen years old and had dropped out of school to join him as a helper. They usually worked at least twenty days a month and together they earned two hundred rupees a day and after spending on travel and food, they managed to take home a little more than hundred rupees. Ramaiah had no land or any other means of livelihood. His only asset was a 20' x 20' site and a small house where his family lived together. His two younger daughters were in school and the mid-day meals they got there went a long way in ensuring that they did not go hungry during the day. Having a mobile phone ensured that the local labor contractor could contact him and keep him posted of any job opportunities that came his way. His mother did not get old-age pension or widow pension and she was informed that she was not eligible for it since she had an adult son who was expected to provide for her.

One of Ramaiah's friend told him that he could apply for a BPL[40]

---

40 Below Poverty Line is a poverty threshold used by the government to identify people as economically disadvantaged and further use it for distributing aid

card, which would entitle him to subsidized food grains at the local 'ration shop'. Ramaiah set about the process of applying for one, and missed many days' wages only to be told by the Taluk office many months later that he was not eligible for one. The reason was that he had truthfully mentioned in the application that his annual earnings were between 30,000 and 40,000 rupees. Little did he realize that honesty had its own consequences in the way the system functioned. He was finding it difficult to make ends meet with rice now selling at nearly thirty rupees a kilo. *Ragi*, his staple food too was no longer cheap and a kilo of ragi cost him around twelve rupees. Vegetables and meat were reserved for special occasions and were becoming increasingly rare. He was perpetually borrowing from the local moneylender who mercilessly charged him around 120% interest. Ramaiah was painfully conscious of his helplessness and found refuge in his evening drink which was making matters worse for him and his family.

I had met Ramaiah at one of the construction sites in Bengaluru as part of my investigations of the state's Public Distribution System (PDS). I had taken upon myself the responsibility of meeting and interacting with a large cross-section of the poor who were deserving of the benefits of the PDS. In my investigation, I had found massive errors of inclusion, but the bigger concern was the fact that there were thousands of genuinely poor families that were excluded.

I was actually amused at the criteria that the state had fixed for determining poverty. As per the state guidelines then, Ramaiah was not eligible for a BPL card as his annual income was much higher than the ceiling of 11,000 rupees for rural areas and because he possessed a mobile phone. How and who fixed these criteria is a mystery to me to this day. A few months later, we were further shocked when the Planning Commission of India, in an affidavit

or offer entitlements. A BPL card is issued by the government to families living below a certain income threshold which entitles them to receive food grains under the Public Distribution System at a subsidized price.

to the Supreme Court stated that any person with daily income less than 26 rupees in rural areas and 32 rupees in urban areas only were considered poor.

How could I explain to Ramaiah that by the state's definition he was not poor and was not entitled to any of the social safety nets that a welfare state had created for families like his? I could not reconcile with my own findings that more than 49% of the families with a BPL card in Karnataka were truly ineligible for the same. Ramaiah, unfortunately belonged to one of those families that had not subverted the system nor was benefited by a short-sighted decision of the state government. The Government of Karnataka in 2008-09 for petty political gains had decreed that any person who submitted a self-declared affidavit of poverty was automatically entitled to a BPL card. What this has translated into today is that nearly 80% of families in the state are considered below the poverty line and are drawing the benefits of various schemes, while 5% of the deserving poor are completely left out.

While this is the reality of most regions of India, our economists and development experts seem to be eternally debating and arguing what would be the best way to define poverty. Should it be a mere monetary measurement of earning around $1 to $1.25 per day or the per capita consumption of 2800 Kcals or something more? Committee after committee has been constituted with no clarity thrown on this matter. In 2010, Oxford University came up with the Multidimensional Poverty Index (MPI) that constituted in addition to lack of income, poor people's experience of deprivation – such as poor health, lack of education, inadequate living standard, disempowerment, poor quality of work and threat from violence. When applied, it reveals that more than 645 million Indians are poor. This leaves India with more than 25% of the world's poverty burden. Eight Indian states collectively have more poor people living here than the number of poor in the entire continent of Africa.

While the appreciation of multiple dimensions of poverty is indeed welcome, all the definitions and calculations are unlikely to help Ramaiah and his family get out of the poverty trap they are in. Poverty also means denial of opportunities. With high inflation rates, social pressures and accumulation of wealth in a few hands, families like that of Ramaiah are condemned to stay poor. The government's anti-poverty schemes, if at all they reach them, would only help in coping with and not getting out of poverty. The trickle-down theory that economic growth through privatization and globalization can help in addressing poverty, despite having been disproved has not been discarded.

Gandhi had said that poverty is the worst form of violence, and by persisting with an economic model that does not equip people to come out of poverty, the state and its agencies, private enterprises and all institutions that supposedly contribute to social and economic progress of the country are guilty of perpetrating this violence. This, even when there is reason and evidence to show that adopting a capability approach can help drive a model of development that allows people to free themselves from the poverty trap.

The fact that there are multiple dimensions of poverty means that addressing poverty is a multi-dimensional effort. While creating institutions and mechanisms that deliver or provide quality education, health-care, water and sanitation, livelihood opportunities, minimum levels of nutrition and financial inclusion to all with respect and dignity constitutes one facet of poverty alleviation, empowerment and building capacities of people constitutes another. The latter includes skill based education, access to credit, humane land and labor reforms, entrepreneurship development, empowerment of women and other marginalized communities and protection from exploitation. Importantly, we must note that the growth and evolution of institutions on the one hand and people's capacities on the other are not mutually exclusive processes. A synergistic partnership of the government, community civil society and a socially conscious private sector can indeed help in meeting the poverty eradication goals in an enduring way. What is needed is a commitment from the state in terms of investment and support in creating an ecosystem where Ramaiah's economic status does not deny him and his family opportunities to partake in the nation's progress and to live a life of dignity.

What does financial inclusion include?

Many years ago, I was traveling to Bengaluru to attend a meeting convened by the state government at Vidhana Soudha, the seat of Karnataka's State Legislature. It was to be a busy day for me with a long list of things that I needed to do on that day and was feeling rushed. I stopped at a wayside eatery to get myself a cup of coffee. I reached out for my wallet to pay for it only to realize it wasn't there in my pocket. It took me a few minutes to gather my wits and sheepishly approach the cashier and explain the situation. He seemed to understand my predicament and having recognized me, agreed that I could pay him on my next visit. I felt distracted and sombre through the rest of my journey to Bengaluru. I was still unsure if I had left my wallet behind at home or had lost it somewhere else. My wallet not only had money, but also my credit and debit cards and my driving license. I suddenly realized how empty and insecure I felt without it. In a strange way, it was my wallet and its contents that seemed to give me not only a sense of identity but also the security that I needed to function effectively on a daily basis. It was then that I realized that what was a one-off, isolated feeling for me is something that millions of our fellow men experience as a way of life itself.

My mind was drawn to an episode when a bank in Heggadadevanakote had closed its operations. It was the only financial institution that the members of the many self-help groups, all indigenous tribal women, transacted with and held their accumulated savings in. I could understand the magnitude of the insecurity these women might have felt when they heard about the bank's closure. This was a rural bank sponsored by one of the larger nationalized banks and had been in operation for a few decades and was located at a distance of about five kilometers from the tribal colonies.

The banks were being pushed by the Government of India to become profitable and hence were trimming down their operations. This meant that the branches not making profits were being closed down systematically and it turned out that most of them were rural branches. The women had come to me seeking my assistance in ensuring that the local branch was not closed. They explained how difficult it would be to travel the additional thirty kilometers to the next nearest branch in order to continue to get the required banking services. It was indeed ironic that they would need to spend forty rupees to deposit their collective weekly savings of hundred rupees.

I met with the chairman of this rural bank and requested him to reconsider closing down the branch. Getting the women to use banks to deposit their savings and for other financial transactions had been an important milestone in the process of empowerment and we now faced the danger of seeing some of the hard work being undone. The bank's chairman for his part, expressed his inability to stop the closure and explained how their priorities had now shifted from social responsibilities to becoming financially viable.

One can imagine the fate of millions of men and women with small savings who depend upon the local banks for their requirements when banks cease to offer the little financial security these people had built for themselves. While this may sound true of rural areas, things were no better in the city of Mysuru too. Last year, a woman who was struggling financially and whose husband had recently passed away met me, seeking help in opening a Savings Bank account in a major bank in the city. Wondering why she needed my 'influence' for something so simple, I suggested that she approach the bank directly. It was then that she recounted her harrowing tale. She had been to a couple of banks located in her area and had similar experiences in both the places. Apart from making her feel unwelcome, she was discouraged from opening an account with them, as she was not a 'viable' consumer. In other words, she was poor and would not have enough money to maintain an account with them. Being poor meant that she was not someone the mainstream financial system would waste its time on. Only after threatening the manager with petitioning the Banking Ombudsman, did he relent and open an account for her.

These examples indicate the state of financial inclusion in a country whose economy is steadily growing and with the third largest purchasing power parity in the world. It is against this backdrop that we need to see the *Pradhan Manthri Jan Dhan Yojana (PMJDY)*, a national mission for financial inclusion launched by the Prime Minister of India a few days after country's Independence Day celebrations of 2014. Speaking at the launch, the Prime Minister mentioned how this scheme was not just about having a bank account but also about helping eradicate financial untouchability. For all those who are born financially included, a bank account may seem to be just another everyday convenience. But for those who are excluded from the mainstream financial system, the experience of exclusion is much deeper than the lack of a bank account or a debit card.

Traditionally financial inclusion is understood as the delivery of financial services at affordable costs to all sections of society, especially the disadvantaged and low-income segments. An estimated 2.5 billion working-age adults globally, who are the unbanked or under-banked have no access to the types of formal financial services delivered by regulated financial institutions. In India, political will has ensured the launch of an ambitious scheme for financial inclusion, and generated enough pressure on the system to respond.

As a result, in nine months since the scheme was launched, nearly 140 million bank accounts had been opened. However, financial inclusion is not just about new bank accounts. The system needs strengthening with opening newer branches in remote and inaccessible areas, novel initiatives like mobile banking solutions including mobile ATM vehicles, mobile banking agents and using post offices as banking institutions.

The mission document of the PMJDY has laid out an implementation plan through 2018, which includes universal access to banking facilities, providing basic banking accounts with overdraft facility and debit card to all households, a financial literacy program, creation of credit guarantee fund, providing micro-insurance to all willing and eligible persons and lastly, pension schemes for those in the unorganized sector. It remains to be seen whether the implementation on the ground would actually align to this plan. Political will and stern dictums can only take the mission forward to an extent. It is important that there is a shift in the mind-set of the banking personnel and all the people in the system to consider the poor as not mere beneficiaries of a government led scheme, but as partners in the progress of the nation.

A bank account would only be the first step in this direction. It does provide a certain social status, a sense of dignity and self-esteem by making the poor, hitherto unbanked, feel important and part of the larger economic framework. Having a debit card may likewise mean a sense of financial independence and empowerment and not just convenience. However, true financial inclusion goes beyond this and includes expanding the capabilities of the poor to make use of these entry points like bank accounts, insurance coverage, and access to credit to climb up the social and economic ladder and not become dependent on a patronizing system. Unless the poor are able to leverage their 'inclusion' into getting better education, healthcare, livelihoods and entrepreneurship opportunities for themselves, the mission cannot be deemed as effective. Data shows that nearly 60% of the 140 million bank accounts created under the scheme have had zero transactions in many months and hence the numbers of banks accounts created are hardly an indicator of the success of the mission. Financial literacy therefore should have been one of the first steps in the implementation process of the mission.

A country like India cannot afford economic or financial policies that do not result in social gains. The question then is whether the financial inclusion mission of the government would be cognizant of and be accompanied by the creation of an ecosystem that facilitates the growth of human and social capital. Without which, the mission's impact would only be superficial and unbecoming of a global economic superpower.

"THIS LIFE IS SHORT, THE VANITIES
OF THE WORLD ARE TRANSIENT, BUT
THEY ALONE LIVE WHO LIVE FOR
OTHERS, THE REST ARE MORE DEAD
THAN ALIVE"

SWAMI VIVEKANANDA

An unending movement

Most processes of development, induced either by the state or non-governmental agencies, are to a certain extent irreversible. The impact of the development interventions and the pace at which their results are evident may however vary and may not really depend on the scale of the intervention itself. For instance, even after decades of having implemented literacy programs in India with hundreds of thousands of people at the task, we haven't achieved a literacy rate of 100%. The same is true of many other programs in various sectors. At the same time, we have seen small initiatives in remote corners of the country evolve into effective vehicles of progress for people belonging the local communities and beyond. A little reflection reveals that these initiatives are those that do not limit themselves to solving immediate problems, but have elements that transform the dynamics on the ground, change the way communities transact with development agencies and have an inter-generational impact. Thus, they may be deemed movements in their own right.

The development journey of Swami Vivekananda Youth Movement over the last three decades is dotted with actions and interventions that have gone beyond addressing local issues to setting precedence, engaging communities in ways hitherto unexplored and helping evolve new perspectives of how the voice of the communities can find more scope and space in the development paradigm. At a personal level as well, there have been defining moments in my journey of development activism, institution building, leadership training, writing and policy advocacy so far, that have helped me grow and evolve my worldview. Every one of those moments, the people behind them and the accompanying reflections and realizations have taught me more about the world and how I engage with it in an ever-maturing manner. In this section, we delve into some handpicked milestones and explore how citizen engagement has rendered them meaningful and impactful while being an unending movement itself.

The inception within

It was February 1984. I was in the third year of my pursuit of becoming a medical doctor in a medical school in Mysuru. Krishna Rajendra Hospital, a district level public hospital attached to this medical school, served as the ground for much of our practical clinical experience before we graduated. I had just passed my pre-clinical exams and had begun clinical rotations in Internal Medicine. The experience of entering a hospital and examining patients was still fresh.

As part of our training, we attended bedside clinics in designated wards of the hospital. One of the patients I regularly saw was a man in his mid-forties hailing from a village in Tirumalakuda Narasipur Taluk, located about forty five kilometers away from the city of Mysuru. I came to know that he was a cook and that he was admitted to the hospital much before we were posted to this ward. He was, however, a known face to the nurses and other para-medical staff working at the hospital.

Every morning we were led into the ward by our professor who was followed by a retinue of personnel in the descending order of hierarchy – the assistant professor, lecturers, post-graduate students, final year students and finally, the third year students among who I was one. Each patient in the ward would be examined by the professor within a minute or so after the post-graduates briefed him about the patient's condition. After this, he would quickly bark out orders that would be faithfully passed over to the ward nurse in attendance. And before we knew it, this patient's examination was over. The patient lying in the next bed would be then attended to. Within twenty minutes an entire ward of around forty patients would be examined and dispensed with. The ward would be enveloped by a bustle for those twenty minutes or so and in this entire melee, we were expected to learn how to deal with patients and treat their diseases.

This particular patient was turning out be a 'difficult case' for the medical team as he was not responding to any treatment. Every passing day, they would hover around him and discuss his condition and after much deliberations, a diagnosis of 'Idiopathic Malignant Hypertension' was arrived at. Everybody felt relieved that they could at least label this 'case' with a title. I was also carried away at that time with the discussions, the intellectualization of disease, treatment and the elaborate logic in finally concluding that we did not know the cause, hence 'idiopathic'.

One early morning, as I walked into the ward, I found the bed that this patient occupied empty. On enquiry, I learnt that the patient had died the previous night and I saw an elderly lady packing up a couple of utensils into a torn plastic bag. I remembered her as the widowed mother of this patient. Courtesy demanded that I console her. As I approached to talk to her, she burst out crying and showered the choicest expletives on me. I was unfortunately the first person with a white apron that she met that morning and she took out her anger at the entire medical profession on me. In the process I discovered some truths that were to grip me for a long time to come. I learned that she was seventy three years old and widowed. They had half an acre of irrigated land near their village that they had sold to pay for her son's treatment. He was the sole earning member in the family and used to work as a cook in marriage functions and other local events. Now she had not only lost her son, but also all hope. So much for 'social and economic' history that we as medical practitioners were supposed to elicit from our interactions with patients.

I suddenly felt that I could not take on the pressure of handling such situations. I was so numb that I did not know how to respond. I tried my best to explain to her that the doctors had done all they could and it was fate that had taken away her son. I told her that he had hypertension that was not responding to the treatment that our learned professors were giving. I explained to her that they had kept changing prescriptions, as he was not responding to any medication that were prescribed.

It was then that she burst out and said that all her son was getting were the prescriptions and not the medicines. She told me that the government hospital had no medicines and she had no money left to buy the medicines from elsewhere. The prescriptions were mere slips of paper and did not translate into any meaningful treatment for her son. And now that son was gone!

I was shell-shocked. I realized that it was not 'Idiopathic Hypertension' that had killed her only source of emotional and economic support. It was 'lack of treatment' born out of poverty. While the entire team in its collective wisdom was discussing his non-responsive condition for the past couple of months, nobody was able to actually understand the root cause. The 'social' and 'economic' dimensions of disease and its treatment was not being taken into account even by the experienced members of the team. I felt lost and hopeless and was wondering what kind of medicine was I being trained to practice.

The next few days were the most difficult ones for me. Feeling inadequate and impotent, I wondered if I had erred in choosing the right profession. I looked around and found no 'idol' or 'role model' to turn to. I had a thousand questions raging on in my mind and had no answers for them and seemed to lack the courage to look for the answers. Ultimately, I realized there could be no real 'outside' support to guide me through the maze and that I had to turn inwards. I had to find my strength on my own and found myself turning to the thoughts of Swami Vivekananda. Not long ago, as a seventeen year old student who had similarly lost the courage to face the troubles of early college life, I had found refuge in the works of Swami Vivekananda. Two small books written by him: 'His call to the Nation' and 'To the Youth of India' had the most enduring influence and had given me the clarity that I was seeking.

However, just being inspired to do something is much different from actually doing something consistently and meaningfully for a long period of time. I had resolved that I would go and serve in the villages of India for their development, but it was this incident at the medical school that helped me realize that systemic changes were required. And such change could only be brought about by a thorough understanding of all factors affecting development. It had to be a slow, organic process and had to have people at its center. I had to be my own role model. I would start an organization that would ask uncomfortable questions and try to find practical and actionable answers.

I would try and start a movement, which would usher in 'ethical, rational and cost-effective' medical care in rural India for people who will be seen as 'people' and not mere sufferers of diseases waiting for treatment. The movement had to have a 'people-centric' approach and in less than a year, some of us had formed a small student led organization that worked in the villages close to the city of Mysuru, before moving to Heggadadevanakote Taluk, where we started to work and live amidst the indigenous tribal communities. This was an organization inspired by the man-making message of Swami Vivekananda, which I hope will continue to serve as a platform for young people to be inspired deeply from within, to come together and work for the cause of building a resurgent India.

The growth of a movement

Our small, inexperienced, student-led organization began its work in the villages close to the city of Mysuru in an attempt to provide ethical, rational and cost-effective health care to rural India. Eventually, we moved to work with the indigenous tribal communities of the district and started functioning from Brahmagiri, a tribal hamlet located about eighty kilometers from the heart of the city. Though we were driven by high idealism, our knowledge and competencies were limited to the field of medicine. Everything that we did, right from registering our organization to living and working with the tribal communities taught us new things and brought in new perspectives every day. As we grew and became more familiar with the communities and their way of life, we began realizing that there were umpteen problems to be solved and issues to be addressed.

We had soon begun appreciating the fact that medical care does not equate to healthcare and felt that unless the communities are educated, our health interventions would not bring any lasting changes. Within a few years, we had moved from make-shift clinics to starting a hospital and operating mobile clinics in order to reach out to more people. Along with it, we ventured into providing education to the tribal children and started a school. Over the next decade or so, the organization had grown, and not only did we have schools and hospitals, our sphere of activities included livelihood projects, organizing and capacity building of tribal women to form self-help groups, initiatives in the areas of water and sanitation and working with persons with disabilities among others.

The growth was impressive and like many other non-governmental agencies, we were responding to what we perceived as problems on the ground, making use of opportunities and financial grants available at the time, to address them. The everyday challenges of managing growth and ensuring the survival of the organization gave little or no time to consciously stay focused on citizen-centric approaches in our projects. It wasn't until we were seriously challenged by the diverse responses on the field that we began to question ourselves, our approach and evaluate the impact of our interventions among the communities. We realized that unless we listen intently to people and their narratives, are open to receiving their wisdom, and introspection, all our efforts would be responses to symptoms alone. We also learned that unless we truly engage with the people, our initiatives could hardly be deemed as a movement.

It was sometime in 1993 that we tried to wage a battle against rampant alcoholism among the tribal men-folk. Since our efforts to dialogue with the men and complaints to the Excise Department about illegal sale of liquor had failed, Puttamma, a brave tribal lady had suggested that we should focus on the people selling arrack. We agreed and did everything from cajoling the suppliers to coercing them and threatening them with legal action, but nothing worked. Having become desperate and at our wit's end, we went a step further and upped the ante. One evening, we went to the temporary outlets selling arrack and started forcibly destroying the liquor. We knew that the retailer could not seek the recourse of law as he himself was indulging in an illegal activity. After continuing to do this for about ten days, three local outlets shut down as they could not sustain the losses. We felt elated at the victory, however short-lived it may have been. As a result of our actions, I was soon threatened, in person, by the excise contractor of the Taluk who had the rights to sell liquor through licensed outlets. In a sense, it was a thrilling encounter, especially to know that our actions had actually hurt him and that I was 'big' enough to be given a threat. But before he turned away, he also remarked that if we truly wanted to fight the menace of alcoholism, we should stop the consumption among the tribal folk, rather than go after the suppliers.

This episode was one of our early efforts at making citizen engagement a tool for progress. Though its success was short-lived, there were numerous lessons to be learned from this experience. In addition to the basic 'demand and supply' lesson of market economics, the experience taught us the importance of coalition building, about the shortcomings of a confrontational approach and more importantly that passion and idealism weren't enough to sustain a movement. Though I must admit that alcoholism among the tribal communities continues unabated, the learning from this and several other incidents went into building our understanding of how we could sustain the outcome of our other activities. We also learned that the success and relevance of many initiatives are dependent on the time and consistency of efforts that go into it. Some initiatives must also evolve into more concrete actions and interventions to become meaningful. Our battle against alcoholism has now gone beyond awareness generation and has taken the shape of running regular de-addiction camps for those addicted to alcohol.

Needless to add, constructive community engagement became central to our understanding of development and became an integral part of many of our activities. We had matured enough to appreciate the 'rights' framework that the development sector was talking about, but also felt that development activities should also have an undercurrent of a 'responsibility' approach. We felt that citizens cannot absolve their roles in ensuring their own development and must learn to partner with the state in moving ahead with their lives. We also redefined ourselves as a 'development organization' and the driving philosophy of our work was to ensure the constant expansion of capabilities of not only the people we worked with but also of ourselves.

We had also restructured our health and education related activities as 'community movements', and when Basamma and Jayamma, the first set of trained tribal nurses started working in our hospital, the health movement had turned a new leaf. Not only had they a better understanding of the communities' health issues, they were the people who could relate and connect to the patients in an altogether different way. As more positions in the institutions were taken up by people from the indigenous communities, a silent continuous movement of expansion of capabilities had begun.

Our work on education started from a cowshed in the Brahmagiri tribal hamlet in 1988, where twenty eight children and a few of us ran a 'school'. Within a year's time, our teams had started reaching out to the communities in far flung corners of the Taluk and soon enough, dozens of first generation school-goers were enrolled in a formal school located on the fringes of a forest. With a view to sustain the education movement, we started an institution for teacher-education a few years later (2006) in the same campus, with the hope that young tribal men and women would take to teaching. When the state introduced the concept of School Development and Monitoring Committees, we joined hands in the strengthening of community participation in the progress of schools. Today, we are witnessing another movement unfold itself in the form of promoting science education among rural school children and teachers with a zeal never seen before.

Right from its inception in around 1992, the Community Development Services, later called Socio-economic Empowerment Program (SEEP) of SVYM focused on facilitating communities to claim their rights and entitlements, rather than deliver any services. The initiatives under this program formed the bedrock of people's campaign for their right to information, the communities' demand of transparent implementation of the Public Distribution System

and livelihood programs for tribal women. Community based rehabilitation of persons with disabilities served to train and empower
one of the most marginalized groups in our society and permanently change their lives for the better.

SVYM entered a new realm in 2002 when it began its engagement with urban communities. The community-based programs
initiated in the underserved areas of Mysuru city brought an
altogether new dimension of citizen engagement. The engagement
with street vendors, the campaigns on making democracy work and
the efforts to involve households in solid waste management were
initiatives, some of which are currently ongoing, where people's
participation has been pivotal to their success. Of particular note is
the palliative care program that is almost completely dependent on
contributions from the communities and the support they extend
to a lean team of care-givers and coordinators. All these are in addition to the leadership training and academic programs specifically
designed to create a committed and skilled pool of young talent to
work in the development sector.

While many of these initiatives are movements in their own
right, they are not without their shortcomings. The biggest one
among them is that most of them are run as programs or projects
for pre-fixed durations and there are always questions of sustainability beyond the project period. We have often reflected upon
these aspects as well, and feel that these are critical questions for
civil society as a whole to answer. What we have learned through
the years is that the project period can be best used to facilitate
an ecosystem that can trigger the process of change in terms of
building people's capacities and molding their attitudes rather than
expect radical changes. Towards this, the team that engages in these
initiatives is usually trained and oriented in a way that ensures
that they are driven by their own convictions, and become change
agents for life, and keep the movement alive wherever they go.

The movement has come a long way, but there is a longer way to go. Its growth needs to be measured not by the number of programs and scale of the initiatives, but by the human and social capital it has been able to build, for all stakeholders: the communities, members of the organization and society at large.

A battle for human rights

There are five anthropologically distinct indigenous tribes who have been living in Heggadadevanakote Taluk of Mysuru District in Southern India for centuries. Categorized as 'Scheduled Tribes', these people are known to have an anthropological history of more than five thousand years. The three major groups are the Jenukurubas, Kadukurubas (locally known as Bettakurubas) and Yeravas while the Bunde Soligas and Paniyas constitute two other smaller groups. Their traditions, cultural values and lifestyles are born out of the context in which they have lived for centuries and encompass their food practices, hunting and food gathering methods, agricultural practices, health issues, learning and education, housing and their system of traditional jurisprudence that determines how they resolve the conflicts that arise amongst themselves and between tribes.

Despite their anthropological distinctions, these groups had been living in peace and contentment in the forests around what is now called N Begur village close to the Kabini River. However, two developments in the 1960s and 70s changed their lives and lifestyles permanently.

The first was the construction of a dam across the Kabini River, which began in the late sixties displacing thousands of families from their settlements. The rehabilitation package evolved at the time comprised monetary compensation and land, which was given to the displaced families. The records available with the Irrigation

Department of Karnataka show that 2,999 families were rehabilitated and 6,221 acres of land were released for this purpose, but 1,731 families were excluded from this process. This included 108 families living in hamlets around N Begur. Though the government admitted that these families had been denied the benefits of the rehabilitation package, all that they were subsequently offered was a one-time monetary compensation of twelve thousand rupees (about 200 US$ at present conversion rates). These families however rejected any monetary package and demanded land for land as compensation. They were forcibly evicted from the forest and eventually settled down on the fringes of the forests in small hamlets.

In 1972, the indigenous tribal communities in HD Kote were dealt a second blow when the Government of Karnataka declared its intent to form a National Park in the Bandipur forests. Though the declaration of intent was formally notified only in August 1985, the forest department personnel evicted all the tribal families from the forests during this interim period itself. This move adversely affected 465 families living in ten colonies within the forests who were brought outside and left to fend for themselves. They were offered no form of compensation. Furthermore, the procedures for notification and declaration of National Parks were not followed by the government, which actually rendered the process incomplete.

The Wildlife Act clearly prescribes the method of notifying the areas and the procedures for relocation of persons living inside the notified areas. As per the act, the department had to notify the formation of the National Park locally in the tribal colonies, make a "Mahazar"[41] of the area, and then prepare eviction proceedings. The then Collector[42] (called the Assistant Commissioner of Revenue

---

41 Mahazar refers to an authorized visual inspection & recording of reality on the ground and preparation of demographic & physical inventory, usually for the record of the court or relevant units of the administration.

42 A career bureaucrat belonging to the Indian Administrative Service and is the head of the executive at the district level

under the present system) had to prepare a list of rights of the people and formulate the rehabilitation package restoring these rights after relocation. In the event of extinguishing of certain rights, he had to clearly notify and adequately compensate the people according to the prevalent policies. It is only after completing this process that the forests could be finally notified as National Parks.

The economic hardships of the tribal communities were compounded by the fact that they had to reside on the fringes of the National Park where collection of Minor Forest Produce (MFP) is not allowed, and as such no traditional tribal occupation is possible. Being forced to live outside the forests, they were denied access to their traditional burial grounds, temples and grazing lands. They were also not permitted to conduct any of their traditional festivities within the National Park's boundaries. With the enforcement of the Forest Conservation Act of 1972, their rights pertaining to their societal customs and traditions, access to hunting and minor forest produce, land rights and livelihood was effectively extinguished without any compensation. It was tragic that this docile and non-violent community who had all along been living with nature, had been left in the cold without a sustainable means of livelihood, pushing them towards extreme poverty and lack of food resources.

In both of these developments, one could witness the government's shoddy attempts at rehabilitation of communities who are already marginalized from the mainstream. Neither the Irrigation Department nor the Forest Department had made any serious attempt to address their real issues. And though we entered this very region almost a decade later, we could see a generation of unsettled communities, uprooted from their past and struggling to cope with life outside the forests.

While it was imperative that action be taken to address the issue and set a precedent for fair compensation and rehabilitation, it was also critical that we view the occurrences as violations of human rights. However, moving the government departments on this premise would not have been possible and hence we petitioned the National Human Rights Commission (NHRC), an autonomous but constitutional body formed by a special act of the Indian Parliament mandated with the task of protection and promotion of human rights. Our petitions, filed in 1996, highlighted both the issues: of improper rehabilitation after the construction of the Kabini Dam thereby leading on to the right of livelihood of tribals being extinguished, and the complete absence of any rehabilitation measures following the formation of the Bandipur Project Tiger National Park, wherein all basic human rights of the tribals had been taken away.

The NHRC appointed Mr. Chaman Lal, a distinguished and retired officer of the Indian Police Service as a Special Rapporteur[43] to look into the complaint, and a series of hearings ensued. Based on his report and the reports provided by state government officials, the commission passed its landmark recommendations in 1998 that directed the state to take prompt action to allot cultivable land to the families within the traditional limits of the tribal communities, provide them with sites for housing along with basic amenities, food grains for a limited period of time and various measures to facilitate education and livelihood. Importantly, the recommendations also included permitting access to the traditional burial grounds, places of worship and allowing the tribals to collect minor forest produce from within the National Park's limits.

However, the NHRC's recommendations lack statutory powers of enforcement and much depends on the political and bureaucratic will and intent for its implementation. It took nearly eight years of sustained negotiation, media advocacy, and activism to get the Government of Karnataka to implement these recommendations.

---

43 A widely respected and highly decorated officer, Mr. Chaman Lal has shown extraordinary commitment to human rights in his career and is a recipient of Padma Shri, India's fourth highest civilian award as well as the Nani Palkhiwala Civil Liberties award among others.

In 1999, the Special Rapporteur himself reported back to the NHRC that the progress on implementing the recommendations were slow and some of the key recommendations were yet to be effected. A statutory committee comprising officials from the NHRC, Government of India and Karnataka State Government, the petitioner and a tribal chieftain was then formed to monitor the rehabilitation process.

Unwilling to leave any stone unturned in the campaign for rehabilitation, we also got the entire cabinet of the Government of Karnataka led by its then Chief Minister, Mr S M Krishna to have its meeting amidst the tribal chieftains at Hosahalli tribal colony. The first of its kind meeting saw tribal chieftains articulate their problems to a retinue of top ministers in the state and demanded that the state respond with immediacy and the seriousness that the issue demanded. Never before had community voices been seen and heard on an equal footing by the people in power. It was possibly the height of community action at work – to have the cabinet respond to the people's demands and immediately initiate all the actions that the NHRC had recommended.

It was by the end of 2005 that the tribals were successfully relocated and the NHRC closed the case in January 2006. The petition filed with the National Human Rights Commission, their subsequent ruling and the delayed, but successful implementation of the recommendations is an exemplar case for the rights of the indigenous people and how they can negotiate with the state to ensure justice gets done. It is noteworthy that this happened even before the UN Declaration of the Rights of the Indigenous people was adopted. This assumes particular significance in a country like India, which has been witnessing an enormous problem of internal displacement and disturbance in the tribal heartland of the country. Ostensibly, the disturbance, often violent, is the result of conflicting interests of the people on the ground and those who consider growth of industries as the primary means of development.

Nevertheless, the government as well as civil society would do well to recognize coercive displacement and conflicts arising out of it as human rights and social justice issues.

For our organization, this battle for human rights was a significant milestone in our development movement. Never before in our journey had we linked our grassroots action to advocacy at the highest levels. It was also an incredible demonstration of how community voice accentuates the process of policy advocacy. Somewhere during this time, the seeds of an advocacy movement based on the strength of grassroots engagement were sown. It was also clear that the state machinery could be made to shed its characteristic disdain and indifference to the voices of the people through constant multi-level engagement by communities and civil society organizations together. Ultimately, it is about getting the state to be respectful of the voice and aspirations of the communities, and that is an unending process by itself.

A grassroots initiative for policy research and advocacy

The year 2009 marked twenty five years of relentless work at the grassroots for an organization which had grown from being just an inspired dream in my mind to a six hundred strong team of mostly young and committed individuals taking charge of various institutions within its fold. The trials and tribulations faced in the initial years to even survive had given way to stability and institutionalization of processes and activities. We not only had presence in different parts of the state of Karnataka, but also had national recognition and presence in the United States of America and the United Kingdom. We had dabbled in multiple sectors of development through different activities, which we believe has impacted thousands of lives, especially those of the indigenous tribal communities and rural populace of the state. We had achieved unique milestones in advocacy like getting Karnataka State's cabinet to convene in the forest, amidst the tribal communities, to address their issues and provide for their entitlements. A battle for the dignified resettlement of more than a hundred tribal families had been won, which could set a precedence in the country for ensuring tribal rights. Our forays in health, education and community development through various interventions had given us a broad base and confidence for furthering the work with the communities on new and emerging issues.

Significantly, the experience of a quarter of a century in

development had revealed how critical it was to engage with communities on a continual basis to ensure that the interventions were contextually relevant and their impacts sustainable. Moreover the appreciation of grassroots perspectives was well entrenched among us.

On a personal level, it was also a time for me to move away from active involvement in the organization for a year or so and let a new leadership take over. I had moved to the Kennedy School of Government in Harvard University to pursue a master's program in Public Administration and the Mason Fellowship in Public Policy and Management. In my 'development' journey, the year and the place was as momentous as it could get, one in which a hard-core development practitioner that I was, could engage with the leading academicians and researchers of the world and where I could juxtapose my experience of ground realities against a limitless sea of knowledge.

This year was also the beginning of a period of reflection and revelation – reflection on the successes and failures of the two and a half decades since the inception of SVYM in 1984, and revelation on new directions to progress in, albeit armed with the knowledge and skills that Harvard could equip me with. During this year, many of my experiences were either validated or challenged by theories, especially the nuances of community dynamics in development that we tend to overlook in program implementation. Yet there were experiences and aspects of centuries old indigenous knowledge that had not found their way in formal academic circles and I was happy that I could contribute my bit to the body of knowledge. On the other hand, I could strengthen my understanding of policy, the dynamics of policy making and contextualize it with how policy making worked in India.

The year at Harvard also revealed the gulf between the world of academicians and researchers and practitioners on how 'development' works. Both their worldviews have strong bases and justifications, but I for one, remain unconvinced that the differences are irreconcilable. In fact, this gulf is one of the factors that facilitated sowing the seeds in my mind, of a new initiative which would have policy research as its core component. The idea was to build an institution that combined policy research work with grassroots perspectives and would therefore need the academicians and practitioners to come together. And the next step would be to further evolve and convert the research evidence generated into a basis for policy advocacy.

I did share the concept with some esteemed friends at Harvard and had mixed responses. Some were not convinced that it would work, but did not discourage me from trying my hand at it, while others could sense a potential in the idea and actively encouraged me. It was to be more than a year before the idea could take further shape and evolve itself and be ready to be launched.

Back in India, the two and the half decades coincided with a period where the relationship between the state and its citizenry had seen many changes. From subjecting citizens to being mere recipients of services or beneficiaries of programs, there was a shift towards adopting a more participatory approach. Civil society, for its part had evolved from being largely limited to charitable initiatives and philanthropy to making itself relevant in the policy space, as evidenced by the increase in networks and forums, campaigns and advocacy groups.

At the same time, economic reforms and liberalization had meant that the private sector had an increasing say and a role to play in development. Given the might and influence of the private sector, policy capture by the industry and their interest groups has been both real and frightening. Successive governments have been competing with each other to achieve double-digit economic growth driven by the voice of the corporate world and crony capitalists, which are together drowning out the voice of the common man. Furthermore, empirical evidence hardly seems to be a basis for policy decisions and actions that affect more than a billion people.

It is against this backdrop that the concept of an initiative that focuses on policy research incorporating grassroots perspectives and evidence based advocacy set about making itself a reality. Grassroots Research And Advocacy Movement (GRAAM) was started informally in January 2011 and became an independent entity in March 2014. The mandate of GRAAM naturally encompasses finding and securing legitimate space for community voices and their development aspirations in the process of policy making and implementation, and thus community consultation is considered as a core activity within the organization, rather than a mere extension of its research or advocacy wing.

Despite the increased space that civil society and the private sector finds, the state in the Indian context remains the prime mover of development. GRAAM aims to enrich the interaction of the key players or stakeholders of development, namely, the state, its citizenry, private sector and civil society through a collaborative approach towards advocating policies that is in the interest of the silent majority who are either anonymous or ignored.

GRAAM aims to change the paradigm where research is driven by a top-down approach by an elite group of people, often without adequate exposure to realities of the developing world at the grassroots level. With experience and skills, we hope to facilitate the process of distilling research questions that emanate from the grassroots level and pursue them with academic rigor. Involving communities themselves at all key stages of the research is also an operating philosophy we aim at incorporating. More importantly, the aim is to work towards ensuring that the results and the body of knowledge generated from development-research is not confined to academic papers and conferences, but is used for policy advocacy in a manner that truly benefits communities.

Since its inception, GRAAM has carried out research, analysis and evaluations in different thematic areas such as public health, sanitation, social security, human development, nutrition and sanitation among others. Along with it, advocacy efforts at the local, state and national level have been undertaken and the organization has been making its presence felt in relevant circles. What is truly important for GRAAM however, is the forging of collaborations with community based organizations, governmental agencies, civil society and development agencies, the academic world and citizenry towards making 'development' a community movement.

While the initiative has crossed significant milestones in a short span of time, there are certain challenges which may take time to overcome. These include the challenge of getting academicians and practitioners to see each other's perspective, translating the perspectives of the people at the grassroots into a language that researchers understand and finding financial support for work that not only looks at a different paradigm in policy research and analysis but also advocacy which needs to be sustained and persisted with over a long period of time to achieve tangible results. More importantly, it needs people who believe in and live the founding principles on which GRAAM has been established, to take the movement forward.

Making advocacy a community movement

Primary Health Centers (PHC), run by the government, are the backbone of the healthcare delivery system in rural India. A majority of the healthcare programs and services introduced by the government are delivered through these centers among which, reproductive and child health services are given high priority. To address the high rate of maternal and infant mortality, thrust is placed on ensuring that women opt for maternity services in institutions rather than deliver at home. Towards this, the state has created PHCs that function round the clock (24 x 7), so that communities can access them any time they need.

Whether these PHCs are sufficiently staffed, stocked with medicines or are prepared to handle complications in child-birth is however another matter. Mulluru village in Mysuru district has a PHC that is designated as '24 x 7' PHC and as per norms is supposed to be manned by two full-time doctors and support staff to ensure continuous availability of service. A couple of years back, however, the PHC did not have even one full-time doctor. There was one doctor in charge of the PHC who was also given responsibilities of another PHC coupled with regular visits to the villages. As a result, deliveries could not take place regularly at this PHC and the primary purpose of designating this health center as 24 x 7 PHC was hardly met. Given the shortage of staff and resources in the public health system in India, the case of Mulluru is hardly an exception. What may be exceptional though is what the communities accessing the services of Mulluru PHC did, with the help of a little training, capacity building and technology.

In a bid to promote community participation in planning and monitoring of healthcare services, the National Rural Health Mission, a flagship program launched by the Government of India in 2005, had mandated the formation of Village Health, Sanitation and Nutrition Committees in all villages and PHC Planning and Monitoring Committees at the level of PHCs. When the Planning and Monitoring Committee members of Mulluru PHC were discussing the issues of their PHC, they complained to the doctor in charge that the people were not getting adequate healthcare services. The doctor for his part explained his limitations and how his commitments and responsibilities were spread. Instead, he urged the people to come forward together and exhort the district authorities to post a full-time doctor in the PHC. The members of the committee deliberated among themselves and decided that they would press their demands in front of a member of the Zilla Panchayat (ZP) they knew. Subsequently, Ms. Bhagyamma Ningaraju, the ZP member, who was apprised of the situation in Mulluru brought the issue to the attention of the Taluk Health Officer. After a period of continuous and consistent follow-up, a full-time lady doctor was appointed at Mulluru, thus meeting a community demand for which the communities led the advocacy efforts themselves. In addition to this, the community members were also successful in making sure that a portion of the funds received by the PHC were spent in procuring anti-venom for snake bites, of which the health center did not have stock.

Similar success stories of communities advocating for themselves were replicated in different villages across Mysuru district. These were the result of an intensive three year initiative undertaken by GRAAM that worked with the communities in rural Mysuru and empowered them with tools for monitoring the services and facilities available in their respective Primary Health Centers. Working with the same committees as mandated by NRHM, GRAAM trained members of more than a hundred PHC Planning and Monitoring committees across the district on responding to a list of questions that indicated the status of services and facilities in their PHCs. This not only involved mobilizing people towards participation in monitoring, but also building their knowledge and understanding what the health centers ought to deliver. The unique aspect of the process however was that the participants had to respond to the questionnaire on their mobile phones. The questionnaires were administered using Interactive Voice Response System and the responses collected were used by GRAAM to rank the PHCs in the district.

The entire project, though experimental, taught us three important things. One is that rural communities have the willingness as well as the capacity to monitor public services and are adept at using technology for the purpose. Second, that community monitoring can be a source of reliable and disaggregated ground level data of the status of public services, which can be used for better planning. Lastly, and most importantly, that the entire process can foster a sense of ownership and encourage communities to take a step further and dialogue with stakeholders, articulate their issues better and drive local solutions. The changes seen at Mulluru and several other PHCs in Mysuru were result of the latter. If people from one village worked with local functionaries to ensure water supply in one PHC so that minor surgical procedures could be done, they have advocated towards getting funds for constructing a fully functional pathology lab in another. In another remote village, a local auto-rickshaw driver has volunteered to provide his vehicle for emergency transport free of cost until permanent arrangements are made. In yet another village, community members even took out awareness campaigns on services available in PHCs and urged people to avail these facilities rather than turning to privately run health centers.

The initiative has provided ample evidence of how communities can be primed to enhance their participation in programs by empowering them to articulate and advocate for their demands. The key question however is whether grassroots voices and empirical evidence based on ground realities would get the prominence they deserve on a consistent basis, especially as the process of advocacy itself has acquired new dimensions over the years. With the increasing involvement of a multitude of influential players including the private sector, international agencies and a discerning media, the policy space is replete with stakeholders vying for attention. Needless to say, political considerations of the establishment also sway priorities. In all this melee, it is the onus of civil society to make sure that community action, constructive engagement and advocacy become a sustained movement.

While we must give due credit to the state and civil society organizations for trying to expand the scope of citizen engagement in various government schemes in what is often called an entitlements or a rights-based approach to development, we still have some way to go before community voices find enough acceptance in the bureaucratic circles. Proactive support of the bureaucracy is critical in making community advocacy efforts relevant and effective, which would essentially depend on the building of mutual trust between stakeholders. When an empowered community swings into action, existing power structures and asymmetries are invariably challenged, giving rise to forces that try and thwart the progress of such movements. With persistence and innovation, these forces can and must be overcome.

GRAAM's efforts to persist with facilitating community advocacy is juxtaposed against this backdrop with the larger aim of democratizing the process of development. Without a doubt, there are gaps and imperfections, and there is a long way to go before we can claim that democratic spaces available have been adequately claimed by communities. However, the potential to reach out to the remote and traditionally marginalized communities and even seek their response has never been so high, thanks to the 'information age' that we live in, and is demonstrated by the project that GRAAM undertook.

With similar persistence from the state, the bureaucracy and other stakeholders, there is no reason why community advocacy cannot evolve into the most critical component of policy making. The state has been providing formal spaces, but the process of creating avenues for citizens to understand and appreciate their evolving roles has been inadequate. This is where civil society can pitch in and take on the responsibility of building capacities of the citizens to ensure that their 'voice' is authentically and pragmatically expressed. Coupled with technology, there is enough potential to convert the age of information into an age of empowerment. All we need is a collective will to drive and sustain community action and move towards closing the gap between people's aspirations and policy outcomes democratically.

CITIZEN ENGAGEMENT –
EXEMPLARS AND REALITIES

Mudalimadiah is a very senior and respected chieftain of the Kadukuruba tribal community. Though I have known him since 1987, we became close only after 1996 when we had started our engagement with the National Human Rights Commission on the issue of displacement and rehabilitation of the tribals in Heggadadevanakote. It was a time when the tension between the forest department and the tribal communities was quite palpable, and even small incidents could potentially turn into explosive situations. The callous and insensitive attitudes of the forest department and the police were making the tribals increasingly restive as the struggle for justice kept becoming longer. Fatigue was creeping in and it was getting difficult to keep the spirits up and the agitation going. The younger generation was showing signs of turning the protests violent and were pushing me to take more visibly strident steps. I also had very little to show in terms of success and my arguments to continue with the non-violent struggle were either weakening or ceasing to have an impact. At times, I was myself feeling low and wanted to give up.

It was around that time that Mudalimadiah came to me. He must have sensed my despondency and offered to join me in the struggle. Despite being a senior chieftain whose words mattered, he had not been involved much in the struggle so far. I was not sure why he wanted to get involved now. He suggested that we spend the next few days traveling from one tribal colony to the other. Not being able to think of anything else, and to keep my flagging spirits up, I agreed. We decided to start our journey the next day and began our march with Jaganakote Hadi, the colony where Mudalimadiah lived. We spent time talking to the tribals explaining the need to keep up the pressure and continue our principled struggle. He coaxed, cajoled and threatened his fellow tribals and also spoke nostalgically of the life in the forest. We moved from one colony to the other and over the next ten days covered all the thirteen tribal colonies in the area. We ate the food that the tribals gave us and slept on the floor in their huts. This was the time I really got to know Mudalimadiah and my respect and admiration for him increased manifold. His father was the local chieftain and he owed all his knowledge and wisdom to him. I found his involvement very difficult to explain. He had no personal stake in this struggle and stood to benefit in no way. He was neither a victim nor would he be a beneficiary later on. All that he seemed to care about was the need to right a wrong.

On one occasion, I asked him why he had joined us and what his motivations were. His answer is a leadership lesson that I still value and treasure. He said that being a *Yajamana* (chieftain or leader) was not a position of authority but one bestowed with a sense of responsibility to the entire community. He said that he had to make sure that he stood up to what he felt was morally right and he felt responsible to compel his people to fight for this just cause. He knew that we stood very little chance if we continued the struggle with only the 154 families that were formally parties to the case. The government would possibly yield only if all three thousand families living in the area got involved. He realized that my charisma and credibility alone was not enough. He had to use his emotional authority and persuasion born out of his traditional position to mobilize the people and get them to join in the struggle. He had figured out that the best way to do this was by getting involved personally despite no personal benefits either to himself or to his family. He knew that he had to live the value of selflessness and experience the uncertainty and insecurity of the struggle to have any charismatic influence on his fellow tribals. He seemed to clearly understand that I as an outsider may have legitimacy in the eyes of the government, but he would always have greater legitimacy with his own people. He was strategic enough to realize that unless we combined our strengths, we stood very little chance in our negotiations with the government. More importantly, he told me that he realized that it was important for me not to lose faith in myself. And the only way he thought he could keep the flame burning in me was by making me live the life of the tribals and get to experience firsthand, their trials and tribulations.

And this definitely worked. I was so moved with their plight that I resolved I would not accept defeat and would keep the struggle going till we reached our goal. Suddenly, this was not a problem that the communities faced alone, but my problem too. Looking back, it was this sense of ownership and understanding of the problem at a very intimate and emotional level that kept me going till the end. True to his word, Mudalimadiah neither claimed any credit nor any physical benefits for all his efforts. Even today, he fondly recollects our time together and the sleepless nights that we spent thinking and dreaming, despite all the odds that were stacked against us.

There is much to learn and reflect upon from the experience and outlook of Mudalimadiah even as citizens around the world are increasingly engaging with the state and its many organs. While the entire experience offers vital lessons in adaptive leadership, it also throws light on facets of citizenship. With nothing to gain personally, Mudalimadiah showed how citizens could step up and engage in a process that brings justice to a much larger community than their own. What is also demonstrated is the cognizance of the larger picture, perseverance of the highest order and the realization that we should never give up on dialogue and constructive engagement. We need to appreciate that Mudalimadiah is at once an ordinary citizen as well as an extraordinary one. Belonging to a community that has seen marginalization and deprivation, he can, on the one hand be deemed to be a victim of the process of development driven largely by economic growth. On the other, he has displayed an exemplary model for citizenship and has done so much more towards promoting citizen engagement than a large number of us do, with more resources at our disposal. Essentially, there is every trait in this indigenous tribal leader, which is needed to build an ideal ecosystem for citizen action.

There are however several questions we must deal with to know whether such an ideal is really possible and how we could work towards it. The first among them is whether as citizens, we are ready to step out of our comfort zones and engage with the process of development deeply. Most urban citizens are beneficiaries of the existing system and enjoy fruits of development that has hidden costs often borne by the economically poor and socially marginalized. From indigenous communities whose forests are sacrificed to unprotected industrial laborers, from people in whose villages our trash is dumped, to victims of industrial pollution and internal displacement, the story of economic growth in countries like India is built on the back of several contributors, who do not necessarily reap its benefits. Citizen engagement towards democratizing the process of development necessarily involves constructively critiquing the model of development that we have benefited from and are engaged in furthering. Can such critiquing happen on a scale significant enough to make development meaningful and enriching for all? Can heads of states, political leaders and captains of industry do it? Can it be done by a large mass of ordinary people, students, teachers and all others on a sustained basis? Would it be too much to ask for all stakeholders to simply engage in introspection, self-analysis and honest critiquing long enough to make a noticeable difference?

There is a crying need for it as well, as we find ourselves in the midst of a development paradigm where the role of multiple stakeholders is ever increasing. I reiterate that meaningful dialogue among the stakeholders – the state, citizenry, private sector, media, civil society and academia can only be sustainable when there is mutual trust. The relationship between and amidst these multiple stakeholders needs to be driven by mutual respect and with an appreciation of interdependence and reciprocity. However, this may involve redrawing boundaries of engagement and roles that stakeholders have traditionally assumed for themselves. Can civil society and people's movements find ways of constructively engaging with champions of industrialization to find common ground that results in viable and sustainable development? Can corporations recognize and accommodate peaceful protests against them and criticism of their practices as valid democratic voices with which they should engage rather than seek ways of suppressing? Multi-stakeholder engagement would require adopting of the partnership approach by all parties involved, but would it be possible without shedding the cultivated biases about each other? Are there any traditional ethics of engagement that are likely to be compromised? These are questions that need collective reflection and sincere introspection.

It is quite natural to expect the state to play the role of a facilitator in building and sustaining these partnerships. It is also obligatory in such a situation for the state to demonstrate its intent and action by protecting the interests of all stakeholders in a transparent and fair manner. Only then can it deepen democracy and democratic dialogue. Why does democratic engagement with people fail to go much beyond election campaigns? Why does the humility and interest in local issues displayed by the political class fade away after the elections? Why are ordinary citizens left to fend for themselves despite elaborate administrative setups at every level?

The state's approach in handling conflicts also needs to be scrutinized. It should not appear to favor those forces and powers that people are dissenting against or resisting, and should play a more active role in addressing conflicts on the principles of natural justice as well as those laid out by the Constitution. We need to bear in mind that citizen engagement is a two way process and it is heavily driven by the responsiveness of the state to citizen demands.

There are on the contrary, several earlier examples of the state of not being very sensitive and testing the limits of ordinary citizens. For instance, survivors of the world's largest industrial disaster in Bhopal, where the leak of toxic gas and contamination of groundwater claimed thousands of lives, have been struggling for justice since decades, mostly peacefully. Despite the fact that the baton of the agitation is now being passed on to a second generation of victims, there is precious little that successive governments in the state and the center have done to bring about any semblance of justice in Bhopal. Whether it is medical care for the survivors, remediation of the factory site or adequate compensation and rehabilitation measures, the state has woefully fallen short of its responsibilities and worse, refuses to assume accountability and do enough to bring the guilty to book. On the other hand, the fight for justice in Bhopal has taken the principled stance of setting the right legal and moral precedence, so that Bhopal like tragedies do not recur. How long should these survivors and activists continue to engage peacefully with a non-responsive state? Is it fair to assume that patience and perseverance – critical traits of citizen action in democracy – are infinite? Can the state move away from its tactic of wearing down the dissenters and look at ways of innovatively engaging with people in resolving long standing issues? After all, the onus of a collaborative approach is as much on the state as its citizenry.

A development paradigm that involves multiple stakeholders is also about giving equal and dignified spaces to each other in the process. What would it take for the powers that be to accord equal space to ordinary citizens? It is rare that ordinary citizens or even citizens' associations get the same status as industry bodies or extra constitutional groups of the elite and the 'eminent'. These are practices that need to be challenged and even if it requires that traditional structures of engagement and power hierarchy be overhauled to accommodate every last citizen, it might be well worth the effort.

We must further appreciate that citizenry or community is not necessarily a homogeneous mass of people and must be conscious of elite capture that happens within citizen groups as well. Furthering democracy is all about constantly finding ways to negate elite-capture and respecting the last citizen's voice. It may need according a new respect to the identity of citizen itself. For which, we must recognize that everyone matters – us, them, you and I, the citizen.

GLOSSARY

Aadhaar

Aadhaar, meaning "support", refers to a 12-digit unique identification number provided to residents in India through a large-scale resident identification program by a Central Government agency called Unique Identification Authority of India (UIDAI). As part of the program, demographic and biometric data of citizens are collected and stored in a centralized database.

Fair Price Shop (FPS)

Fair Price Shops are retail outlets where food and non-food items distributed under the Public Distribution System in India are made available to the consumers. (See PDS below)

GRAAM

GRAAM (Grassroots Research And Advocacy Movement) is a public policy research and advocacy organization based out of Mysuru, India. Initiated as a unit of SVYM in January 2011, GRAAM has been functioning as an independent registered Trust since March 2014.

Gram Panchayat (GP)

Gram Panchayat is a village level institution that forms the lowest tier of the three-tier Panchayati Raj system. Comprising elected representatives of a village, the Gram Panchayat is responsible for local self-governance and the delivery of most development programs introduced by the state or central government.

Heggadadevanakote, HD Kote

Heggadadevanakote, often called HD Kote is a Taluk in Mysuru district in the southern Indian state of Karnataka. It is geographically one of the largest Taluks in Karnataka and is home to several indigenous tribal populations. Though the Taluk is rich in natural resources, it is among the most backward in terms of human development and socio-economic progress in the state.

Jan Lokpal Bill

Jan Lokpal Bill translates to Citizen Ombudsman Bill and refers to the version of an anti-corruption legislation drafted by civil society organizations and anti-corruption activists in 2011. This draft is different from the Lokpal and Lokayukta bill passed by the Indian Parliament in December 2011, which was criticized by opposition parties and civil society alike, as weak and ineffective. Arvind Kejriwal, the Chief Minister of Delhi in 2014 tried to introduce a version of the bill in the Delhi assembly unsuccessfully. (See below)

Lokayukta

Lokayukta, meaning appointed by the people, is an anti-corruption ombudsman appointed by the state governments in India vested with powers of investigation on matters of corruption and mal-administration

Lokpal, Lokpal Bill

Lokpal, meaning caretaker of the people, was a word coined in 1963 and refers to a constitutional ombudsman for inquiring into corruption allegations against public servants with a large jurisdiction including members of Parliament, bureaucrats, current and former ministers, and the Prime Minister, once s/he has demitted the office. The Lokpal and Lokayuktas Act, also known as Lokpal Bill, was first introduced in the Indian Parliament in 1968 and after several attempts was passed by the Lok Sabha in 2011 and defines the contours of the institution of Lokpal, a body with both investigative and prosecution wings.

Mahatma Gandhi National Rural Employment Guarantee Act / Scheme (MNREGA)

MGNREGA is a social security measure introduced in India through an act of the Indian Parliament in 2005, which guarantees to the rural population of India, employment with wages for a minimum of 100 days in a year for one adult member of the household willing to do unskilled manual labor. Employment under MGNREGA is a legal entitlement to eligible citizens, who are to be given an unemployment allowance, if no suitable employment is provided. The onus of implementing the act is on the Gram Panchayats.

Making Democracy Work

Making Democracy Work was a campaign launched by SVYM with the support of Association for Democratic Reforms to increase voter awareness and encourage responsible participation in elections. The campaign was conducted in two phases, in the months preceding the Legislative Assembly Election of Karnataka in 2013 and before the Indian Parliamentary elections of 2014, in Mysuru district and Mysuru Parliamentary constituency (which included parts of the neighboring Kodagu district) respectively.

National Rural Health Mission (NRHM)

NRHM is a flagship program launched by the Government of India in 2005 aiming to improve the healthcare delivery system in rural India, which resulted in a significant rise in the public health expenditure of the country. The stated goal of the mission was to improve the availability of and access to quality health care by people, especially for those residing in rural areas, the poor, women and children and thus focused on strengthening reproductive and child health services.

Panchayati Raj, Panchayati Raj Institutions (PRI)

Panchayati Raj is a system of local self-government prevalent in the Indian sub-continent comprising elected bodies at the village, block (Taluk) and district level which are vested with the responsibility of planning and implementing schemes for economic development and social justice in their areas. The core philosophy of the PRIs is democratic decentralization with devolution of powers and responsibilities. The 73rd amendment to the Constitution of India provided constitutional sanction to the PRI in 1992.

Public Distribution System (PDS)

The Public Distribution System (PDS) of India, one of the largest food security initiatives in the world, is a nation-wide program under which, highly subsidized food grains are distributed to the poorer populations by the government. The procurement and distribution of food grains and some non-food items, such as kerosene, is handled by the Ministry of Food, Civil Supplies, Consumer Affairs jointly with the state governments through retail outlets called Fair Price Shops. (See FPS above)

Right to Education (RTE) Act

The Right of Children to Free and Compulsory Education Act or Right to Education Act (RTE) is a legislation enacted by the Parliament of India that provides a constitutional guarantee of access to education for all children in India between the ages of 6 and 14, and puts the onus for the same on the states. The Act came in to force on April 1, 2010.

Right to Information (RTI), RTI Act

The Right to Information Act is a powerful legislation passed by the Parliament of India in 2005, which conferred on the citizens, the rights to obtain information from public authorities. Under the provisions of the act, the competent public authority must respond to the application requesting for information within a period of thirty days.

Social Audit

Social audit is a process of reviewing official records of the state, usually in public with the participation of civil society organizations and citizens, to ascertain whether the money spent under development schemes align with the expected outcomes on the ground. The audit may also include other provisions of the said schemes. The origins of the concept is attributed to *Mazdoor Kisan Shakti Sanghatan,* a Rajasthan based NGO.

SVYM

SVYM (Swami Vivekananda Youth Movement) is a development organization founded in 1984 by Dr. R Balasubramaniam with the aim of providing health-care services to the tribal population of Heggadadevanakote Taluk of Mysuru and has since expanded its scope of work to include education, community empowerment, training, consultancy, and research.

Taluk

Taluk, also known as Tehsil, is an administrative division comprising a group of villages and usually a town, which also serves as its administrative center. Also called blocks in some contexts, a group of Taluks constitute a district. The local self-government at this level is called Taluk Panchayat and it forms the middle or second tier of the three-tier Panchayati Raj system in Karnataka. A Taluk is comparable to a county, though there are certain dissimilarities.

Zilla Panchayat (ZP)

Zilla (District) Panchayat is the top-most tier in the three-tier PRI system and is responsible for district-wide rural decentralized governance. The ZP consists of democratically elected members, representing different rural constituencies of the district and is headed by one of these members, elected as the President of the ZP. The bureaucratic head of the ZP is the Chief Executive Officer.

Do you have questions and comments about citizen engagement, democratic participation or development paradigms that are discussed in this book?

Do you have experiences and narratives to share – of citizen engagement or any related theme that could complement or contrast those that are mentioned in this book?

Did this book help foster discussion and dialogue in your circles, classrooms or elsewhere and has resulted in better appreciation of citizen engagement or raised newer questions?

Share your thoughts and reflections: **citizen@graam.org.in**

GRAAM

Grassroots Research And Advocacy Movement (GRAAM) is a public policy research and advocacy organization based in Mysuru, India that focuses on undertaking research that incorporates grassroots perspectives and advocacy based on empirical evidence using a collaborative approach. GRAAM's body of work is a unique attempt to bridge academic objectivity and development dynamics on the ground on the one hand and to place community voice and evidence at the forefront of public policy making on the other. It further aims to enrich the interaction of all stakeholders – the state, citizenry, civil society, private sector, media and academia towards making development a truly participative and democratic process.

www.graam.org.in

THE AUTHOR

Having embarked on his journey in the development sector by living and working for several years among remote forest based tribal communities in the southern Indian district of Mysuru, **Dr. R Balasubramaniam** (Balu) is a widely respected development activist, leadership trainer, thinker and writer. He has uniquely been able to combine a vast development sector experience with studying and teaching at the world's leading schools of policy and development including Harvard and Cornell Universities. He has also been a special investigator for Lokayukta Karnataka in addition to holding membership & consulting positions in government bodies and commissions, academic boards and development agencies.

Dr. Balasubramaniam, the founder of Swami Vivekananda Youth Movement and Grassroots Research And Advocacy Movement embodies a rare blend of grassroots and macro perspectives on development and policy through his multi-faceted experience of more than three decades, which is well reflected in the book.